ALSO BY STEDMAN GRAHAM

Move Without the Ball

Teens Can Make It Happen

You Can Make It Happen

Build Your Own Life Brand

DIVERSITY
LEADERS NOT LABELS

STEDMAN GRAHAM

FREE PRESS
New York London Toronto Sydney

FREE PRESS

A Division of Simon & Schuster, Inc.
1230 Avenue of the Americas
New York, NY 10020

FREE PRESS and colophon are trademarks
of Simon & Schuster, Inc.

Designed by Kris Tobiassen

For information regarding special discounts for bulk purchases,
please contact Simon & Schuster Special Sales at 1-800-456-6798
or business@simonandschuster.com

Manufactured in the United States of America

10 9 8 7 6 5 4 3 2 1

Library of Congress Cataloging-in-Publication Data is available.

ISBN-13: 978-1-4165-4273-5

I want to dedicate this book to Mary Graham, my mother, and my sister Anita. You are both pillars of strength and examples of how you can keep going and never give up. It is the stuff you can't buy. To my pillar of strength, Oprah, you don't set the standard, you are the standard.

This book is also dedicated to all of the people who have come from all over the world to make America what it is. The strength of your spirit and your leadership is what has made this country great.

Acknowledgments

I would like to acknowledge my publishing partners for "making it happen" with this book that I have enjoyed putting together. I want to thank Carolyn K. Reidy, for her dynamic leadership throughout the years. A special thanks to my editor Dominick V. Anfuso, who has believed and stuck by me and allowed me to be creative, and also thanks to his capable assistant Wylie O'Sullivan. I want to, of course, thank my agent, Jan Miller, about whom I can't say enough. Your expertise along with your determination and your big heart put you in a very unique category. Thanks to Shannon Miser-Marven for your support in helping me throughout the years, and a special thanks to Steve McLinden, who has done a fine job helping me in developing the research and putting this book together; it's been a pleasure working with you. I hope you are as proud of this book, *Diversity: Leaders Not Labels,* as I am.

Contents

Section 1. Diversity in the Twenty-first Century

Section 2. Programs from the Past

Section 3. Transformation

Why This Book?

As an educator and speaker, I am grounded by a fundamental message that I have conveyed over the years to organizations who've sought my help in building platforms for the personal and professional growth of their people: *The world is a collection of unlimited wealth and resources. Often, we limit our potential by moving in our own small circles because of our fears. If we change the way we view the world, there is nothing we cannot accomplish.*

This sentiment is important to me because it represents a different kind of thinking—a thinking that gives you the confidence that you can be, do, and accomplish anything.

Diversity: Leaders Not Labels is about changing the way we think about our possibilities, which is not just an option these days, it is a requirement. We are moving into an ownership society where we must become more accountable for how we are viewed and defined. The question can sometimes be ask "Who owns you?" The answer needs to be "I do."

Today we are challenged to keep reinventing ourselves while not limiting our potential as we work within the system. Growth and change do not always come easily because so many of us are programmed to stay in a box based on how we've been labeled.

We end up stuck in a routine, doing the same thing over and over, locked in place with no growth. While education is important, we get fooled into believing it's the principal tool for growth, as we memorize, take a test, get labeled with a grade and regurgitate information to teachers. Asked a couple weeks later what we learned, we've probably forgotten.

So how do you grow? How do you reinvent yourself when your core base is weak and you don't know who you are? How do you build that foundation for thinking and developing if you haven't defined yourself and taken control of your life? The millions of people of all races, backgrounds, and nationalities who have lost their personal control need to recognize the importance of regaining self-ownership and then learn a process to achieve that goal.

The law of the jungle is more applicable today than at any other time in our history: only the strong survive. As the world becomes more global and technology brings us closer together, our environment has become more diverse. Your transformation from a follower—or someone's label—to a leader in this competitive climate is a must.

And you must move quickly or you may not have a job. Tens of thousands of traditional manufacturing jobs have been lost and thousands of others are being outsourced or have been rendered obsolete. The business world is transitioning to a technology-based model. As job security, pensions, and other safety nets disappear, there are countless thousands who will find themselves thrust back in the workforce as free agents. People are also living longer, retiring later, and using up life savings that they once thought would be enough.

What is our twenty-first-century world—the Information Age—demanding? Talent, skills, performance, excellence, and results. A college education may get you in the door for an interview, but the real question will always be What do you bring to the table? What marketable skills do you have? Where does your expertise lie?

The twenty-first century is looking for people who can move past their history and into their imaginations. In the past, the business world's focus has only been on people who could help it improve the bottom line and increase sales. But the type of person who will succeed in this new work environment is one who can also transcend race and build relationships—someone with a spirit of cooperation who is tolerant of others. This environment will require people who think before they react and who understand the consequences of their actions. It calls for self-respecting people who feel good about where they came from and don't apologize for who they are. And it calls for people who will continue to grow and develop and who will bring value to themselves and those they represent.

In *Diversity: Leaders Not Labels*, we will explore different cultures and their experiences to help you understand that everyone has had his or her own challenges and issues. You'll see that the process for growth and transformation are the same for everyone and that hard work, sacrifice, talent, and self-motivation are the tools for the future. In this book, we want to help people to transform and to respect others' uniqueness by first cultivating and respecting their own.

What makes us all equal is that we all have twenty-four hours. What's the question? "What do you do with your twenty-four hours?"

Best regards,
Stedman Graham

Diversity in the Twenty-first Century

ONE

The Lessons of Whitesboro

First, I must tell you about an instrument of change in my own life, a man who was central to my transition from race-based thinking, a man whom I never met.

As I grew up in the 1950s and early 1960s, racism still infected the black communities of our country like a plague. It was more conspicuous in the South, but it lingered in the North as well, and New Jersey was no exception.

Whitesboro, New Jersey, was much like other black towns that sprang up across America in response to antiblack violence and segregation. It was also my hometown, my sanctuary, as I grew up. In areas surrounding our town, blacks were still being openly disrespected, shut out of jobs, and treated like second-class citizens. A kid growing up in Whitesboro felt a little more insulated from this day-to-day despair.

But the story of this unique town's founder, George Henry White, dates back far before my time there. White, in fact, was born a full century before me. But his legacy lives on in my heart and the hearts of the thousands who have dwelled in Whitesboro over generations.

White was a visionary man who devoted his adult life to securing the most basic rights for the underrepresented. He understood the power of leadership and education in overcoming the label of "second-class citizen." Born in Bladen County, North Carolina, in 1852, he spent much of his childhood in servitude, working as a slave in the humid forests of the region to harvest the precious pine gum used in the making of turpentine and many other common products. He toiled from sunrise to sunset for the benefit of wealthy slave-owning families in a youth he called a "struggle for bread and very little butter."

White was thirteen years old when slavery ended. He knew that extreme poverty was inevitable for most former slaves, so he rededicated his life to helping the legions of newly freed yet disenfranchised men and women gain access to the only thing he knew could give them hope: education. He worked his way through a teaching school and then Howard University in Washington, D.C., later earning a law degree. He got elected to a seat in North Carolina's House of Representatives, where he fervidly petitioned for increased funding of African American schools. He would serve as district attorney in New Bern, North Carolina, and later as state senator.

In 1894, White took an even bolder step, running for a seat in the U.S. Congress. He lost but was not deterred and clawed his way back to capture the post two years later. A brilliant orator, White made impassioned, classic speeches about the prejudices and brutality plaguing African Americans in the South. White, as it turns out, was the last former slave to serve in Congress, and by 1898 was the only African American remaining in the House of Representatives.

White went down in history as the first to introduce an antilynching bill, illuminating his colleagues on the sobering fact that 80 percent of the people who were being lynched across America in his time were African Americans. But White's bill stalled in the Senate, and similar House bills met the same fate over the next hundred years. On June 13, 2005, an antilynching bill finally passed the U.S. Senate, with language apologizing for the many previous failures to address the violence that killed thousands in our nation's past. White's century-old quest for contrition from his country was finally realized.

But that's just one part of the George Henry White story. Back in 1900, White began to realize the hopelessness of pursuing a third term. North Carolina's legislature, you see, had ushered through legislation that banned blacks from voting. White saw the writing on the wall and knew his days in the House were numbered. Before leaving, White delivered his final congressional speech, the historic "Defense of the Negro Race," in January of 1901, refuting white-supremacist claims and recounting how racism had unduly influenced our country's legislative process. He promised that blacks "will rise up again some day and come again" and then spoke his parting words "on behalf of an outraged, heartbroken, bruised and bleeding people—but God-fearing people—faithful, industrious, loyal people, rising people, full of potential force."

White's moving farewell speech was in many ways a new beginning.

For years, White felt that African Americans could thrive if given the chance to build their own communities. Blacks in the South—while free in theory—were still being afforded precious few civil rights when he left office. So White hatched the idea of developing an all-black town somewhere in the North.

Not long after his departure from Congress, White and a handful of loyal friends bought 1,700 acres of a former slave plantation on the southern tip of New Jersey—in Cape May County—to birth a town that would soon come to bear his name: Whitesboro.

Early settlers with names such as DeVane, Stanford, and Spaulding—the latter, my ancestors—came mostly from North Carolina, followed later by families from New Jersey and surrounding states. Following White's lead, the settlers realized that education was the connection to power, prosperity, and respect and were anxious for their children to develop a strong intellectual foundation and a sense of racial and community pride. A school and church sprang up, as did a lumber mill, grocery

stores, a hotel, and other businesses. Largely removed from the prejudices, negative labels, and other racial obstacles of the day, Whitesboro
grew to forge a distinctive and rich cultural identity.

I became a part of this legacy when I was born to Mary and Stedman Graham in Whitesboro in 1951.

Though we were insulated there, there wasn't a person born in
Whitesboro who didn't come to realize how the town was perceived once
they traveled outside its city limits—and that there was a specific set of
slurs and labels reserved exclusively for people like them, people like
me. There was a saying in south Jersey: "Nothing good comes out of
Whitesboro."

So we grew up knowing we were different. And in different mediums,
we heard the same message over and over: "You are not as smart as
whites." Though we lived in a town with few resources, we were lucky
to be blessed with several outstanding, no-nonsense teachers at my
school, Whitesboro Grammar School. These teachers took it upon themselves to sternly prepare us for the rough ride ahead. The memorable
lessons taught by Charlotte Harmon, Alice Jones, and Ines Edmunds
reverberate even today. They insisted we focus heavily on reading, math,
and science and impressed upon us that we had better know our lessons
well. If we didn't, they would make darn sure our parents knew all about
it—immediately. Our school only went up to fifth grade, and we knew
we'd soon be attending white schools outside Whitesboro's city limits. In
essence, the teachers were telling us, "We don't want you to go up to those
white schools and embarrass us."

So we grew up with a sense of pride in Whitesboro. We respected our
family members and we respected the elderly. We didn't tolerate name-
calling. However, there was an unwritten rule when I was a kid that white
folks weren't allowed in Whitesboro. It was our haven—our respite. If
white people ventured into town, we chased them off, with the exception

of sports teams that would come down to our fields for home games. When that happened, it was a huge event in the community. Because we constantly felt we had to prove ourselves, we knew we had to be twice as good as white kids to get anywhere, and we weren't going to let these guys beat us on our own ball fields. Pride was all we had and pride took over.

My family worked hard to develop the few resources we had. We struggled like many families did in Whitesboro. My father was a painter and carpenter, but he would not teach me those skills because he did not want me to follow in his footsteps. He wanted me to get my education and grow up to be something else. Because my father was a person of color, he couldn't get into a painters' union. So he had to take on all the odd jobs that no one else wanted. All his life, he had a sense that he was being put in his place, and that his family was being put in its place too.

You could count on reading anything negative that happened in Whitesboro in the newspaper. Incidents that would have never been significant enough to write about in a white community became news when they happened there. Sometimes that negativity was a self-fulfilling prophecy. A number of my friends and classmates who had been good, smart, and athletic kids turned on themselves and got involved with drugs. Some were sent to prison. They were looking for a way out and often didn't find one.

Students were bused from Whitesboro to attend Middle Township schools, where I attended an integrated high school. I was a drum major there, a basketball player and founder and president of a club called Betterment Through Understanding (BTU). I was a Boy Scout and was treasurer of the freshman class. As active as I was, I still hadn't come to fully understand the real value of education.

I was always pressing, always trying to convince myself and others that I was good enough. We were living only in the moment because we had to, most of us thought. As I grew to high school age, I internalized a lot of rage. We had been disrespected for so many years that we felt we had to prove ourselves. Our self-esteem had been diminished. That led to physical intimidation. When we were about fourteen or fifteen, several of us would walk into places outside Whitesboro and feel all eyes in the room on us. We'd turn around, look menacingly at them, and bellow, "What are you looking at?"

But most of our parents in that era "stepped in line." They bought into this whole race-based consciousness and were unwittingly enforcing it. They were always aware of how they carried themselves, and hence, so were we. I had to watch every move I was making because I felt I was always in jeopardy; I had to work at fitting in. Away from Whitesboro, the realities of racial bias were hitting me hard, and I would often internalize racial incidents that went on in my high school. There was always some race-based controversy.

As a person of mixed Native American and African American ancestry, I was light-skinned. Because of that, I suppose, I was a little more palatable to white America than some. But "light-skinned" became a self-attached label and a stigma for me. We were all subdivided into differently shaded groups that often marked how much money, culture and, class we were due. And I felt I was naturally entitled to a little more because of the lightness of my skin. I might even be able to get into doors that darker-skinned blacks could not, I thought. It took me a long time to realize that such race-based thinking was to my detriment. Instead of focusing on my academic merits, I was becoming class-complacent and class-conscious.

There was a time in my life when I said to myself, "I don't know how a black man makes it. How do I get past the labels and the psyche of the world and all this separation?" After all, our world is a place that seems to shout out, "We are going to put up all these obstacles and create a system that labels you and keeps you locked in with bars all around you. We know you're probably not going to make it, but if you somehow do, well, that's amazing. We might even throw you a bone if you get out."

I never imagined in my wildest dreams that success in life was more about understanding who I really was. For the longest time, I thought I would be happy if I got lucky enough to get inside the white world *even just a bit.* Of course, there were certain unwritten rules you had to follow to accomplish this. You had to be subservient in the way you talked and acted. You had to walk softly. Otherwise, you would be knocked back into your place.

Obviously, we felt as if the whole world was telling us what we could and couldn't do, and it seemed the bar had been lowered for African Americans. When counselors told us to "stay in school," they usually didn't mean "go on to college." They just meant we should finish high school. We were even told by a school counselor that we shouldn't plan on going to college to become a doctor or lawyer or dentist because those weren't the professions that people of color could choose.

Hundreds of years of labeling and programming have affected millions of lives. Imagine how many legacies would have been different if people were free to believe that they could be anything they wanted.

But it was a little different for me back then. I was headed to college. Blessed with athletic ability, I led my basketball team in scoring. I had scholarship offers from schools all over the country when I was a sophomore. I even thought, "Maybe I'll be able to play professional sports." For a lot of us, sports represented a way out. But we knew in the back of our minds that some of us weren't going to make it out that way. We didn't have a lot of vision beyond that one hope.

Sometimes, when I wasn't in school or playing ball, I would help my mother clean houses in white, upscale beach towns such as Stone Harbor and Avalon. Their owners would arrive for the summer season in new cars and hang out at the beach all day, tanning and indulging. Then they'd come home and order in food. My mother and I would look at each other in amazement at this exotic lifestyle, as if to say, "What is all this?" These houses were huge. They seemed like a fantasy land—like Disneyland. Coming out of Whitesboro, I found the experience even more surreal.

That's how I grew up in the fifties and sixties—in a disjointed, divided world. I had no control of my long-term thinking. It was all too common for many in that era to grow up reacting emotionally instead turning on the brain.

I realize in hindsight that what I was trying to do was fill that hole in my heart. I think about this often, especially now that one of my main roles is teaching other people how to process their upbringing and move forward based on a nine-step methodology—a process that I will address a little later in this book in a leadership and diversity context.

There is a huge dichotomy between what I knew when I was growing up and what I know today. My life has taught me that many people are still stuck in these "places" and aren't really able to take more control over their lives and explore the great possibilities they hold. Over the years, I turned all those things that happened to me and to my family into motivators, never forgetting and never getting comfortable.

Fortunately for me, my parents were there to encourage me to never quit and to do my best always. And in much of Whitesboro, that same spirit of determination prevailed, passed down through the generations from our town founder, Mr. White.

If that same spirit of determination is not in you, you're going to have a tough time making it in this changing, demanding world. The only way you can move forward through this life is with a passion for what you do, a lifelong commitment to develop your skills, and an ethic of hard work.

Eventually, I would return to Whitesboro a changed, more enlightened man. In the interim, I learned much more about the psychology of race-based thought and race-based exploitation. I have been visiting Africa annually for years. On one such occasion, I was with a U.S. group visiting an impoverished village, accompanied by members of a charitable organization, who were mostly white. As we waited in a van listening to a member of the organization talk about the pathetic state of some of these poor, malnourished African kids, one of the folks said, "It is sad how the people in this region are so poor." I remember replying, "Let's talk about where this poverty really came from. Consider all the rich farmland that was once in this part of the world. If all those people from everywhere else around the world didn't come in and feed off this land, mine the diamonds, and take all the minerals out of the ground without putting anything back, it wouldn't have happened. They plundered all the resources. Before you knew it, the whole continent was divided up like a pile of treasure. They weakened the foundation when they did this. They left no infrastructure behind for the people whose resources they stole. That seemed to be their plan all along. It was a setup. Then people came over trying to help and ended up taking control. What we need to do is create opportunity and move forward—to leave something meaningful behind. People here couldn't even farm their own land or feed themselves. They couldn't benefit from the wealth of their country because of this negative outside influence. Isn't it a shame that we have all these starving children now?" As the folks from the charity sat there listening, their eyes sort of widened, and one said, "You know, you're right. That is what happened."

When you realize what your legacy is—and frame it in a way that helps you understand how you got where you are—you can achieve perspective on your life, I came to understand. Instead of feeling diminished by the past, I position it this way: "What can I learn from that past that can propel me beyond it?"

That's the first step toward transcending—moving past the constraints that others have imposed on you—and transforming into a more productive and accepting human being. I realized that this challenge was twofold for me: I needed to reprogram how I felt about myself and see myself for my own unique qualities, not someone else's stereotypical view of me. As a rule, people don't tell us how to do this.

Too many of us just look at past oppression and mistreatment and say, "Woe is me."

Of course, struggle is not unique to people of color. Almost all of us have endured some sort of major struggle. We are the same in that way. What we all need and want is love and respect and someone to care for us.

That binds us. We just come from different cultures—be they Whitesboro or White Plains—and many of us see our lives only from that vantage point.

It took me a long time to move out and away from the bad things in my life and embrace the good things—to transcend my past. Only from that point on was I truly able to move into my imagination and my possibilities and my identity. But it's an ongoing process. If I execute it every single day, it will be reinforced and much more effective. If I don't, I fall back into old traps.

Continuing reinforcement of positive values is paramount to anyone's transformation.

Though my home base is now in Chicago, I return to Whitesboro several times a year. Over the years, the more I thought about what I've received in wisdom and perspective from this distinctive New Jersey town, the more I knew I must give something back. So when I came back to town in 1989, it was with an agenda: to form a nonprofit grassroots organization called Concerned Citizens of Whitesboro.

In the original spirit of community pride instilled by town founder George White, I felt an obligation to aid in the town's social and economic revival. Through Concerned Citizens, we members seek to raise money and form partnerships with the county, the community, and several local organizations to help restore the vitality of Whitesboro. We have added streetlights, fixed sidewalks, and shored up aging infrastructure, as well as built voter registration programs, senior citizens' programs, family support services, recreational programs, scholarship programs, and other educational opportunities for youth.

Our overall goal is to help "the Boro" transform, stay vital, and welcome systemic change that will lead to stronger leadership and a healthier community.

Through Concerned Citizens under the leadership of a man named

Bernie Blanks, and with the support of the committee and local residents, we continue to make a concerted effort to preserve and promote local pride in the town's unusual history and distinctive character. From the beginning of this effort, we wanted to stand up for our community and help give it representation.

Without that reinforcement, advocacy, and commitment, Whitesboro could descend to the status of a "second-class citizen" town. We owe it to George Henry White and the original settlers of Whitesboro to honor their founding ethics and not let that happen.

TWO

Diversity at Work

The real voyage of discovery consists not only in seeking new landscapes but in having new eyes.

—MARCEL PROUST

Diversity is more than just being "politically correct." It is not, as some say, a political football. Diversity is about our role in ultimately moving civilization forward and freeing ourselves to forge alliances we'll find beneficial and profitable in navigating our changing world.

Increasingly, this world's newly empowered people are commanding respect from the business and corporate world. In turn, savvy businesses are finding unlimited economic and competitive advantages in the creation of socially diverse corporate structures. The art of knowing the wants, needs, and aspirations of diverse customers pays off. It enables businesses to develop services and products that are tailor-made to their customers' needs and whims.

Businesses, organizations, and people that demonstrate an understanding of the differing cultural, linguistic, and religious requirements of existing and potential customers will have a natural advantage over those that don't. That's not conjecture. I deal with dozens of companies who tell me this over and over.

Diverse workforces can help their businesses build sales by matching the demographic of their customers with that of their own frontline staff and sales force. Customers are more inclined to trust salespeople who have similar cultural characteristics. Businesses and organizations can ill afford to ignore any new opportunities—especially these! Similarly, minority customers and minority business owners are understandably reluctant to trade with companies that have a reputation for discrimination. More and more, all businesses are questioning the policies and practices of those companies that they trade with.

There's more competitive motivation for businesses to recognize differences in their hiring practices and policies. That strategy is not only good for growth of the bottom line, it is good for employees' confidence in the decision-making processes of their employer. Team members feel included. In fact, studies consistently show that companies with constructive diversity cultures realize much higher levels of motivation, teamwork, satisfaction, service quality, and sales growth.

In contrast, employees in companies with more passive diversity cultures often feel more pressure to think and act in ways that will avoid conflict and please superiors. They are less likely to act in a manner consistent with what they believe needs to be done to operate the company more effectively. In such cultures, strong ideas and beliefs, as well as good judgment, often take a back seat to rigid rules and bureaucracy. As a result, these cultures experience more turnover and unresolved conflicts, and their employees experience lower levels of satisfaction and motivation. In other words, savvy corporate leaders see a diverse culture as an asset to be developed and nurtured—and make sure they have the climate to support it. They transform their enterprises and they reap the benefits.

We're coming to grips with several other realizations in our society. We're dealing with a lot of "free agency." People are building their own personal brands, building their own Web sites, and building their own opportunities. We are dealing with constant change. There is a lot of reprocessing going on. We're exporting a phenomenal amount of work to China and India. There are plant closings, funding cuts, corporate downsizings, and well-publicized failures of leadership locally, regionally, nationally, and internationally. There's global warming, new stressors, new health and aging issues. People are living longer. The world is changing faster than our understanding of it. Young people are entering jobs and leaving them so fast they aren't around long enough to get employee benefits. A lot of people have to go back to work, or they remain on the job years longer than their forebears did.

How do we deal with all these changes? How do we process them? We start by being more accepting of people of all backgrounds, being more flexible, more tolerant, and more fluid.

On a personal level, we must constantly reevaluate ourselves and move with the times. Sometimes you just have to grit your teeth in a certain situation and learn how to deal with it. You needn't win every confrontation. Remain positive, understand where a person is coming from, and create an engagement.

The sooner we understand our cultural baggage, the sooner we can leave it behind and move forward to put our talents and differences to their highest and best uses in this diverse world of ours. That's what transcending and transforming in this context are all about. We are *transcending* our old racial barriers to move with the flow of humanity and are *transforming* into a valuable commodity to our families, to our workplaces, and to the world—all through this process.

Once we've reflected on where we've been, where our ancestors and peer groups have been, and what they have endured to get where they are, we can move on. By identifying what controls and labels people have placed on us and what controls and labels we have internalized and placed on ourselves, we construct a launch point, a foundation from which to propel ourselves away from the trap of race-based thinking.

The next logical step in shedding that baggage is to move into the next natural progression of your life. Of course, it's always easier to acknowledge the need to move on than it is to do it or to ask the question, "How do I change?"

We best start this metamorphosis by redefining ourselves on our own terms. By identifying and escaping from negative stereotypes and behavior patterns that we may not even have realized were present in us, we are breaking invisible chains—chains that shackle us as we wind our way through this complex and competitive labyrinth of life. With an open mind and some self-reinforcement, we can discard negative labels to clear a pathway to success and leadership, whether in the workplace, in the home, or in society.

We've all been wronged, unfairly labeled or put in a box of someone else's construction—some of us much more than others. But if you can't let the past go, then it is you who may be let go—from a job, from business or personal relationships, or from a path of destiny that has opened up to you.

Today's global business environment doesn't accommodate negative thinking or an entitlement mentality. It is a world that won't wait for you to work through your self-pities or break out of your shopworn stereotypes. It will continue to spin and leave you far behind, should you choose to remain on the sidelines crying "foul."

The privileges once reserved only for affluent, non-ethnic males are now available to everyone. All you need to know is how to access them.

The world is transforming, and we must transform with it. It demands that we have a vision of our future unclouded by the past. The world is changing at a faster pace than at any time in history. While racism is still alive, its pulse is weakening in civilized society. You can see it happening. Twenty years ago when someone cracked a racial or sexist joke in public, people still laughed. Ten years ago there may have been some laughter, but it was probably nervous laughter. Today there is dead silence. Fewer and fewer people give a second thought to interracial couples and friendships or the presence of ethnic groups in every walk of life.

As the world comes together, its people are coming together.

THE RULES HAVE CHANGED

Your peer group isn't what it used to be. "Difference" is not only acceptable, it is the norm. The minority is now becoming the majority, as you'll
see in coming chapters. It's clear that in America the word *minority* will
eventually be applicable to white men and women.

This is your best chance yet to use all your talents and differences and
connect with the world. Because the new workplace is about working
with people with similar interests—not just with the same race, background, or orientation—your new allies may be different from you in
their cultural and ethnic backgrounds, but you will still share a common-
ality of purpose: to succeed and contribute and earn a decent living.

What else is changing about the world? Everything! The United
States is no longer an island in itself anymore. Today we all can be linked
in milliseconds with people halfway around the world. This convergence
of humanity makes you a global player, whether you know it or not. You
may not be an international traveler, or even much of a domestic traveler.
But the world is still at your fingertips—as close as the buttons on your
keyboard or phone and the remote control on your TV.

You will have to be ready, however. You will need the right set of leadership skills and the right attitude to thrive and even to stay alive in this
new world. There may be civil wars raging, continuing conflict in Iraq,
ongoing instances of terrorism and famine and natural disasters, and
other big blips on the screen. But nations are joining forces like never before to solve the world's problems, especially after September 11 and the
terrorist bombings in London and other parts of the globe. Despite the
isolated instances of conflict and hatred, it's an exciting time to be alive.
Airports are full of people of all cultures heading toward unprecedented
opportunities in the emerging markets of China, Russia, and Latin America and to the far corners of the earth—places that will be demanding increased attention from a globally aware generation.

People want to explore and travel and grow their businesses abroad and are doing just that as new routes and pathways open up all over the world, and as international airfares drop. You can feel the energy and the urgency around this country and around the world. With the population diversifying all around you, it is not a good time to be stuck in your old thought patterns or mired in a constricting environment not of your own making.

You might or might not be a person of color or another minority, but regardless of your background, you are part of a diverse tapestry that is rapidly enveloping the world. And it's not just a phenomenon happening overseas. No matter where you sit in this country, the changes are apparent.

The boss who hired you last year may be quietly planning to move your manufacturing post to Malaysia next year. That cable TV customer service rep you spoke with last night probably made your account changes from a phone bank in India or the Philippines. The construction firm that employs your spouse may have been late to finish recent jobs because other fast-growing countries have been outbidding the United States for materials, as those cultures race to upgrade their enormous infrastructure and get in step with the rest of the world. Or it may be that your colleagues are struggling to digest all the curious customs, cultures, and cuisines of all those new workers who were hired in your international department recently—the ones who may accelerate past you if you're not ready to evolve with this new workforce.

While nationalism is still alive, provincialism is dying. Fewer and fewer of your countrymen care whether their clothes, cars, computers—and colleagues—are "Made in the USA."

What's more important now is who can put together effective workforces and make products better, cheaper, and more accessible. Never in our nation's history have so many companies had customers and coworkers with so many differing backgrounds. But if you thought the cultural changes of the last decade came at a breakneck pace, then buckle yourself in for the next decade.

TRANSCENDING YOUR RACE

Why is transcending—or "rising above"—your own race so important?

There's an infinite number of opportunities, both at home and abroad, waiting out there for those who can grow past their stereotypes and prejudices. Today there are fewer barriers to advancement and fewer excuses than ever for being left in the wake of other people's successes.

Most big companies would like to help you better advance through the ranks, especially if you've come from a disadvantaged background. And there are some great diversity programs that are helping accomplish that. But your employer, I must tell you, can't afford to babysit you through this process much longer. Several companies have confided that very thought to me. They might say, "After a point, we just can't afford to take care of diverse people the way we'd like to. Most of our time and energies are going into staying competitive with the global markets. But Stedman, I really don't think I can come out and say that . . ." But I can and do.

Another message is ringing clear through all of this upheaval. International commerce, as an entity, really doesn't care about race, creed, gender, or sexual orientation. Its main concerns are survival, profitability, and control of its own destiny.

Companies can create progressive and meaningful diversity programs within their organizational structure, but they can't afford to create social agencies.

Some of those little extras you've come to count on are ending up on the cutting-room floor when budgets are squeezed. Everything is performance-based now. More than ever, it's the strongest and leanest who will survive: any soft links can literally break or corrupt the chain. It is up to you to use your difference to your advantage. But don't expect special treatment because of it.

A MORE LEVEL PLAYING FIELD

The first step to swimming in ethnically diverse waters is learning how to respect and work with the cultural differences of your coworkers who are from varied backgrounds and foreign lands.

You and your company should not merely tolerate diversity. You should celebrate it as a core strength. Leveraging those differences for a competitive advantage will pay off for everyone involved—both at home and abroad. Leaders who can respect, understand, and motivate coworkers from different races, cultures, age groups, and countries without an enormous amount of prompting will be worth their weight in gold.

When I say "leaders," I am not just referencing your boss. No matter what station or level you occupy in an organization, you become a leader when you set a positive example. Then others start to see you as a leader—including that boss. Eventually, you become a boss—your own or someone else's.

In many ways, the expanded global marketplace is an equalizer. It offers advantages to people of all backgrounds and persuasions. It puts them on a level playing field. They're not labeled or marginalized as frequently as in the past. There's little time for that. Like those commercials said, "Just do it."

There's less time to make excuses as well. The time has arrived to abandon unreasonable expectations. It's time to buy into the program, if you haven't already, and take control of your life. Instead of making the system work for you, you have to find a way to work through it, by leveraging your differences.

TIME TO ACT

There are many ways to break through professional barriers. Take a long, studious look at your company. See how it competes, where it competes, and with whom. Study it like a CEO. Become conversant with the market and your specialty or subspecialty. Put your newfound knowledge to work. Figure out what your own role is now, and do your best to determine what it might be in five years—and what you'd like it to be. Try to make the two ends meet. Plot a course.

Chances are, your company and the market it caters to will change along the way. And you should be ready to change with it. Like it or not, a competitor somewhere in the world is probably knocking off the product you're producing now or selling your service cheaper. There's little you can do to stop that. But you can devise a plan B, a plan C, and a plan D.

The following steps to success work for individuals and company leaders alike who want to be a part of a diverse and global force:

- Reject negative labels—yours and others'.

- Celebrate and embrace difference and diversity as a core strength.

- Stay in motion. Anticipate change.

- Study the market and be a step ahead of it. Look down the road five years.

- Change how you market yourself—to your employer, customers, or other businesses. They are changing. You are changing.

- Travel abroad and study a second language. Unlike the United States, most countries are bilingual.

- Redefine goals and aspirations in the context of your new knowledge.

Rethink, refine, redevelop, reinvent, retool, rise above—and regularly. Do your homework. Global expertise requires sensitivities and nuances that are vastly different from our domestic ways. Study different cultures. Keep abreast of international news.

Remember, it's not just about trade. It's about understanding people, as well as their traditions, interests, and backgrounds. The best businesspeople study a culture thoroughly before they immerse themselves in commerce there.

There's an all-too-common realization among first-time international business travelers that becomes apparent within a few hours of their arrival at their destination; their ethics, attitudes, and expectations don't play in Poland or Peru or Pakistan. If you haven't advanced past your own labels or stereotypes, it's much harder to be open to other cultures and forge international friendships.

Consider going back to school. Companies are looking for educated, flexible, and diverse job candidates who can think critically and who have an international perspective. Workers must develop skills that are internationally recognized so that they can move with minimal complication between today's jobs in our country and jobs in another country tomorrow. Customize your program.

After all, you are the face of your company or organization. As part of a workforce serving consumers and other companies around the world, you must be prepared to meet business needs in every way possible. The success of your company's ventures at home or abroad—including whether a potential customer overseas chooses to continue to cultivate a relationship with your company—will depend increasingly on the individual whom your company chooses to represent it—you!

CHANGE WITH THE WORLD

The economic machine that has been the United States for generations has slowed down somewhat in recent years as other countries have produced similar or better-quality goods at cheaper prices, while the dollar has weakened. Because of the growth of the Internet and other technology, jobs are being farmed off with relative ease to India, China, Russia, Thailand, Malaysia, the Dominican Republic, the Philippines, and many, many other places.

A lot of money and work is leaving the country. America can expect a migration of more than 3 million knowledge-based and service jobs overseas by 2015, according to Forrester Research. Seventy percent of those positions are predicted to go to India alone.

Meanwhile, a brisk building boom and elements of Western-style capitalism are sweeping across China and other once-closed countries, as they strive to compete around the world with goods and services. It's evident that once people get a taste of independence and free trade, there's no stopping them—or deterring them from diving into that ocean of commerce where you are currently swimming.

The European Union continues to solidify as well, becoming a greater force. And in the developing world, all countries now have technology that will help them jump into the fray. In fact, more young people than ever are entering the global labor market. In the developing world alone, it's estimated there will be 700 million new entrants to the labor force between 2002 and 2010.

Civilization is not slowing down. People are hungry to make a better life for themselves and their loved ones, and they are progressing. International airline routes are expanding. English, which used to be the most widely spoken language in the world, has now been overtaken! (See chart.)

Languages Most Widely Spoken

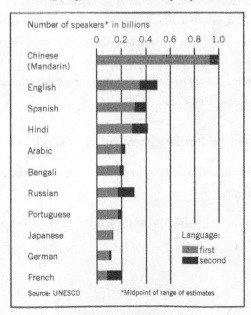

Number of speakers* in billions

Language:
first
second

Source: UNESCO   *Midpoint of range of estimates

Recent data from the United Nations Economic and Security Council Organization (January 12, 2005) yielded some real surprises about the number of speakers of a first and second language. In the United States, speakers of both English and Spanish are rapidly increasing as both immigrants and their children learn English, and as English speakers realize the economic, social, and political value of learning Spanish.

Bridging the language gap is no longer just an issue for coastal, border, and big-city school districts. The multitude of languages spoken by new immigrants—and not-so-new immigrants—is a challenge everywhere. At some schools, over a hundred languages are spoken.

While English arguably remains the language of international business, that doesn't mean that commerce is conducted in an Americanized way. International etiquette as well as local customs and cultures dictate a different and more diverse modus operandi. Learn those and get ahead of the game.

While the debate rages on in the United States over affirmative action programs, your assurances of a quality role are increased by full participation in an ethnically diverse worldwide workforce, where there is no such debate. And it's a safe bet that if you take care of diversity in the U.S workplace, you will be able to adjust to other cultures in the international marketplace and thrive as a result.

Don't look for others to help move you forward until you've initiated the process yourself. Remember:

- Get rid of the cultural baggage, but keep the culture.

- Transcend the old barriers and transform into a valuable commodity.

- Redefine yourself—but on your own terms. (We'll explore this in more detail.)

Discussion Questions

1. What does it mean to be American today compared to the time when you were born?

2. Other than traveling and working abroad, how can your company adopt an international perspective?

3. What is the difference between becoming a more diverse person and "transforming"?

4. How can workers in the United States reinvent themselves to compensate for the ongoing loss of jobs to laborers overseas?

THREE

Writing Our Own Labels

Labels, by nature, try to define what's on the inside. They're handy for choosing canned goods at the grocery store, counting grams of fats and carbohydrates, buying clothing, or shopping for a new computer. They're useful because those who attach them are familiar with the contents of the package.

They do, after all, save you the time and trouble of examining the merchandise more closely. When you read them, you know what to expect, what the product offers and doesn't offer, and whether it will meet your expectations and needs.

Not so with people. Labels placed on individuals by other people seldom reflect what's on the inside. But they often do dictate how we view people and, ultimately, how they view us. From the time we are young, we are told by parents, peers, neighbors, teachers, and the media what our potential is and what the potential of others is—often based on our color and position in life. We are programmed. And a lot of us just accept that programming, consciously or subconsciously, as "truth in labeling." Those stereotypes become self-perpetuating. So in this sense, we program ourselves.

It's not that labels are inherently bad. Rather, it is the associations and assumptions attached to them that can either serve us well or do us a grave disservice. Tennis great Martina Navratilova said it well: "Labels are for filing. Labels are for clothing. Labels are not for people."

The reality is, labels have been used throughout history to separate people, generally with an underlying motivation of gaining power and profit—the classic "divide and conquer" strategy. Most labels limit us and limit others. There's an old, cynical saying: "How can you really hate something unless you slap a label on it first?"

"UNLEARNING" MISTREATMENT

No matter how well-meaning our labelers are, they have probably lived their lives under the constraints of their stereotypes, which in turn were drawn from their peers and role models, with those seeds probably planted in their own formative years. The majority of us, at least to some extent, experience some form of systematic mistreatment or discrimination when we are young, whether through harsh discipline, the invalidation of our feelings or our intelligence, or the discounting of our abilities. As a result, we tend to internalize these negative experiences as "the way things are," then dish out more of the same to others who are close to us.

DISCRIMINATING DEFINITIONS

The terms "discrimination," "prejudice," "stereotype," and "label" can hold different meanings in different situations. For our purposes, here are a few clarifying definitions:

LABEL/STEREOTYPE An exaggerated image or distorted "truth" about a person or group allowing for little or no social variation or individual difference, usually passed along by peers, family members, or the media. Such labels are often used in an attempt to arouse prejudice in an audience by targeting or reinforcing its fears or biases. Labels can be negative or positive but are more often negative.

What we are seldom told is that *we alone make the decision whether or not to break away from these patterns and accept these labels!* The process of undoing these learned behaviors involves consciously interrupting this cycle in our day-to-day interactions.

I can't recall a major entertainment vehicle in recent years that captured the essence of this subject better than the Oscar-winning film *Crash.* The movie dares you to assume that you know its characters by their race and the roles they're playing—until you are confronted with evidence to the contrary. All of its characters are defined by racism in some capacity, either theirs or someone else's. The writer/director, Paul Haggis, illustrates that it's not a black-and-white world we live in; he portrays many people who are quick to label as otherwise caring individuals. As several people from diverse ethnic groups crash into each other—literally or figuratively—they learn about the extent of their biases and the potentially disastrous effect they carry.

The message is clear: any one of us can jump to conclusions based on stereotypes and can even pay a heavy price for it. There are also numerous real-life examples. In the case of police or the military, for example, such deep-seated biases may affect life-or-death decisions. We've seen numerous instances in recent years where law enforcement per-

PREJUDICE Literally means "pre-judging." A prejudice can be an attitude, opinion, or judgment about a group or an individual and is often accompanied by fear, hatred, or ignorance. It is learned usually from a close circle of friends, acquaintances, family members, or peer group and is directed outward to another group or individual and can be passed along to the next generation. Prejudice is largely negative and often acquired with other biases early in life, surfacing in ethnic jokes, slurs, and discrimination.

DISCRIMINATION An act of prejudice against a person or group, ranging from insults to hate crimes to predatory or exclusionary policies or legislation. It often begins with prejudices, negative stereotypes, or negative events that involve a person or many persons of a group and are thus falsely held to be representative of an entire group.

sonnel shot people of color who were mistakenly assumed to be holding guns.

When we stop to think about it, we realize that hatred and intolerance aren't always at the root of prejudice: social conditioning usually is. But where there are cultural differences, tension is possible—even inevitable. Yet ultimately, the virtues of respect, understanding, and hope can also follow too, as we confront the root of our biases and the biases of others. It is a discovery process for all of us, as we interlock or interact with diverse people, a process that forces us to come to grips with hidden feelings and learn about ourselves and why we are what we are.

"It's an odd life we live . . . in a city that uses freeways and wide boulevards to divide people by race and class," said director Haggis in an interview (movienet.com, 2005). "We spend most of our time encased in metal and glass; in our homes, our cars, at work. Unlike any real city, we only walk where 'it's safe'—those outdoor malls and ersatz city blocks we've created to feel like we're still part of humanity. We no longer truly feel the touch of strangers as we brush past them on the street." Actor Don Cheadle's character sums it up in the early moments of the film: "I think we miss that touch so much," he says, "that we crash into one another just to feel something." *Crash* reinforces the conviction that we are living in a culture that's reaching out to its diverse components to make those connections and to bridge those gaps—to work through, and ultimately from, our differences as points of strength.

It's no surprise that this acutely introspective tapestry of racial isolationism won the Best Picture Oscar in 2006. The movie's producers took a big chance in proceeding with this risky work without the support of a major studio. But the film obviously struck a responsive chord with viewers and the Academy.

Crash helped take the discussion of racism to somewhere it hasn't been. Now we need to take it another step further.

ESCAPE FROM YOUR LIFE BOX

Many people regard their confining life boxes as safe places where they can live out their days unbothered in secure, personal comfort zones, knowing what to expect. In truth, their self-expectations, both personal and professional, are diminished in the process. They have stopped growing. The truth is, no one is holding you back but yourself—unless you allow them to.

This isn't a time to hide under a shell or put your life in the coast gear. It's a fluid and diverse world out there that demands flexibility, uniqueness, self-confidence, and understanding. It's also a fascinating period in which we're living. Other nations, it appears, are starting to gang up on the United States. Americans traveling abroad have discovered this in recent years. There's a growing perception that—at least for now—we're not the be-all, end-all leader of nations that we once were.

But if you're clear on who you are and what you represent, you can thrive in the changing world and even be an important interface for it. This isn't a culture for people to just wander around in aimlessly, with no real connection to the world. Pawns are in ample supply. Queens and kings are not.

But do you have the tools for the job? Can you assert yourself to become a part of this fast-changing world? Can you find a common ground with the rest of humanity without giving up your identity or ethnicity?

Absolutely!

The rules have changed. The playing field is leveling out. The privileges once reserved only for the nonethnic male are now available to everyone. All you need to know is how to access them.

CHANGING FACES IN WORKPLACES

Diversity is literally changing the face of the American workplace. The 2000 U.S. Census was an eye-opener, especially for the business world. Half of all consumers under age forty are now people of color. What's more, three-fourths of all American children under ten years old are also people of color. That's a lot of diverse consumption coming down the pike, especially as this group matures, and catering to it will require a lot of specialization and cognizance of consumption patterns that are unique to the varying ethnic groups. Products and marketing philosophies must adapt. Corporate America can't afford to ignore this momentous demographic change.

But those numbers don't show the entire economic and demographic outlook. The buying power of minority groups has been steadily rising and has nearly doubled in the last decade. New entrants to the workforce will be 70 percent women and people of color by 2008. Workers of all backgrounds and nationalities are merging into the global marketplace here at home. Businesses are challenged by a talent shortage and the need to integrate cultures into the national workforce. Increasing competition means they must reach out into new markets or find fresh ways, and fresh faces, to serve their existing markets.

You may have noticed another recent workforce trend: the erosion of employee loyalty and employer loyalty. Company leaders are struggling to formulate a vision that is palatable to workers, while workers are struggling to remain loyal in the face of reorganization and outsourcing. Ironically, this estrangement comes at a time when the need for recruitment and retention of diverse and talented individuals is at an all-time high.

It's up to you to bridge that gap. Multiculturalism in this global marketplace is here to stay. That means there will be plenty of opportunities to go around. And you won't have to become a member of anyone else's culture to play a crucial role in this round.

One of the keys will be learning how to mold your uniqueness into something positive for those around you. You will have to figure out how to assert your own distinctive identity and determine how that tracks into the widely diverse American society of the present and future.

In 1968, during another time of great transition and transformation in our country, humanist and author Jerome Nathanson observed, "The price of the democratic way of life is a growing appreciation of people's differences, not merely as tolerable, but as the essence of a rich and rewarding human experience." That axiom has never been more relevant in this country than it is today. When you clearly define yourself without sacrificing your own culture, you serve your community and your ethnicity in the process.

Unlike at times in our country's past, your uniqueness today is a commodity, not a liability. The world is not only awaiting your contribution, it is demanding it and rewarding it. At the same time, you will have to be adaptable to other cultures, mind-sets, and generational styles. But you can land a more rewarding role in that world and still play the role that you know best—yourself.

ADD TO THE MOSAIC

America has long prided itself on being a "melting pot" of different cultures and races arriving from distant lands. "Give me your tired, your poor, your huddled masses yearning to be free." Those poetic words of Emma Lazarus inscribed at the Statue of Liberty embraced immigrants for generations as they came to our country with the intent of somehow blending into our culture.

But are we truly a melting pot?

There were two schools of thought on this question as our nation grew into the twentieth century. One was that as all the factors holding each ethnic group together—shared language, customs, intramarriage, occupational specialization, segregated housing, fear, discrimination—disappeared, so would the cohesiveness of the ethnic groups. This was called the "assimilationist" theory, which gave birth to the old melting pot analogy that we hear in the media with some frequency.

The other held that America was becoming more of a mixed salad than a melting pot. It said that over time, the varying cultural groups could coexist—peacefully or otherwise—without becoming part of a more uniform American culture and sacrificing their traditions and customs. So these folks, who were called "pluralists," felt that true ethnic assimilation was not inevitable.

And history, it appears, has ruled in favor of the pluralists—two centuries and several decades after the birth of the nation. The passage of time, as well as more refined research and analysis of census data, show they were the more visionary of the two groups. The ingredients in our nation's pot have never really melted. We have not become a homogeneous nation—despite Wal-Mart and other mass merchandisers of sameness! Commodities are a necessity for everyone's survival, of course. But customization is the way you adapt and thrive in the changing world. It needs diverse components to succeed in its transformation.

As it turns out, the groups that form America haven't lost their unique and discrete identities in favor of an end product of uniform consistency and flavor, as they would have done in a true melting pot. Instead, each ingredient of this "salad" contributes positively to the whole while maintaining its integrity. People whose families have lived in the United States for generations still identify with one or more ethnic groups. They also say they're Americans!

It's now clear that "ethnic" and "American" are no longer mutually exclusive terms. Even with increasing rates of intermarriage, greater social mobility, and a stronger push by various ethnic groups to the suburbs (once considered the domain of only nonethnic, or "mainstream" America), there's still a motivation for people to identify with their ethnic labels. Former president Jimmy Carter saw it happening long ago and summarized America's population with these words: "We have become not a melting pot but a beautiful mosaic. Different people, different beliefs, different yearnings, different hopes, different dreams."

Not to say some "melting" hasn't occurred. While Lady Liberty did not say check your cultural baggage at the door, many immigrants did leave parts of their customs, languages, and traditions behind when they cast off from the shores of their homeland. They wanted to blend in, to be part of this great American society. They learned English or made sure their children did. Some stopped speaking their native languages in the home.

If they practiced a religion different from the mainstream Protestant faith, they usually kept it to themselves or within their own ethnic enclaves. Some chose to exchange their religion for Protestantism. They began to dress more "American." They didn't want to be labeled immigrants or foreigners. In their own minds, as well as the minds of most mainstreamers of the time, these Old World practices would stand out as a stigma. Through the generations, many immigrants have willingly adopted the look and speech of white Americans if they felt their chances of getting a job or a loan or gaining entrance into a college, club, or other "traditional" American organization would improve. This is a fear-driven assimilation strategy—and, unfortunately, sometimes necessary for survival. But a lot of cultural wealth is lost in this process. That needn't be the case anymore.

Labels have slowly changed through the decades as well. No longer are such terms as "Oriental," "colored," "crippled," or even "Indian" along with their negative associations and assumptions—in use as commonly as they once were. Americans now realize that it's okay to have multiple identities. The degree to which third- and fourth-generation families still list a heritage other than American on the census is a telling sign of the meaning and importance of ethnic identity. They may consider themselves American, but also Italian or Catholic, or they may call themselves Christian or Jewish Americans.

You can't always change how others view you because of the associations they have with the labels you've been given. But you can change yourself. It's not about blending in. It's about reaching deep within your soul to find your essence. And it's not just about embracing a new label. Understanding diversity means appreciating both the big and little things that make a culture unique.

Ethnicity is a source of pride—not something to be hidden anymore.

You can "assimilate" without sacrificing your heritage or identity, and hopefully do so without becoming disrespectful or cynical. You'll have to in this emerging global economy. Remember those principles on the way to transformation, but don't sacrifice your identity in the process!

That's how you will become a leader—of others and yourself—in the twenty-first century.

Discussion Questions

1. Is America more of a melting pot or a mixed salad?

2. What labels have you been given throughout your life? Please note which ones are related to qualities or conditions you were born with and which to conditions you have lived under.

3. Of these labels, which ones hold you back and which ones move you forward? Which have helped you find or create success?

4. Explain your identity in five labels.

5. Do you see these labels as positive or negative? Explain.

Programs from the Past

An Introduction

Like a pane of glass framing and subly distorting our vision,
mental models to determine what we see.

—PETER SENGE

Derogatory labels and language aimed at ethnic groups and other minorities are slowly vanishing from our lexicon, but a tendency to stereotype still remains deeply ingrained in many people.

Why is this?

We know it is programmed behavior. But we also know that a fundamental characteristic of the human brain is its ability to distinguish friend from foe by sorting out people. Thus, it is in our nature to group. But over the years, that grouping *instinct* can easily become a grouping *impulse,* especially with constant reinforcement from peers, coworkers, family members, television, advertisers, and other media.

So while grouping is natural, racism isn't. Human beings are not born with it. Racism—as well as other forms of bias against people who seem different from us—is caused by a mixture of misinformation, ignorance, fear, and negative social conditioning. Cultural and physical differences in human beings don't trigger labeling and other bigotry, but they're often used to justify it.

In our "Programs from the Past" section of this book, we'll show how cultural programming in America began well before readers of this book were born and how various inaccurate or distorted labels and generalizations have been passed down through the ages—to all of us. We'll look at how leaders of these groups have emerged to transcend those barriers, exploding myths and stereotypes along the way while ultimately helping pioneer our changing views of people of difference.

There's never been a time when this kind of information has been more critical, as people of all persuasions and races converge in the U.S. workplace and our global economy. As of 2004, about 35.7 million U.S. residents—or more than 12 percent—were born in another country, according to the Pew Center. Similarly, data from Canada indicate that recent immigrants represented nearly 70 percent of that country's labor force growth between 2000 and 2004, according to Pew.

To include as many of these diverse people as possible in this section, I've selected the following groups: Native Americans, Latinos and Hispanic Americans, Asian and Pacific Islander Americans, African Americans, and Arab Americans. In the chapters on "Gender Wars," I'll focus on women, gays, lesbians, bisexuals, and transgendered people, plus in another chapter I'll examine the case of people with disabilities. Certainly, many other ethnic and cultural groups also face discrimination and mislabeling, and I hope to include some of them in a future work.

Knowing how and why these scenarios occured in our history and what their impact has been on humanity will help give you added insight as well as a launching point—a place to step away from those old boundaries so that you can better understand yourself and realize what's important and distinctive about you—the qualities that can make you a leader, not the product of another person's label.

ANCESTRY OF U.S. POPULATION BY RANK

As this ancestry chart illustrates, the fabric of the United States is
more diverse now than at any previous point in the country's history.

RANK	ANCESTRY	NUMBER	PERCENT	RANK	ANCESTRY	NUMBER	PERCENT
1	German	42,841,569	15.2	22	Spanish	2,187,144	0.8
2	Irish	30,524,799	10.8	23	Filipino	2,116,478	0.8
3	African American	24,903,412	8.8	24	European[1]	1,968,696	0.7
				25	Welsh	1,753,794	0.6
4	English	24,509,692	8.7	26	Asian Indian	1,546,703	0.5
5	American[1]	20,188,305	7.2	27	Danish	1,430,897	0.5
6	Mexican	18,382,291	6.5	28	Hungarian	1,398,702	0.5
7	Italian	15,638,348	5.6	29	Czech	1,258,452	0.4
8	Polish	8,977,235	3.2	30	Korean	1,190,353	0.4
9	French	8,309,666	3.0	31	African[1]	1,183,316	0.4
10	American Indian[1]	7,876,568	2.8	32	Portuguese	1,173,691	0.4
				33	Greek	1,153,295	0.4
11	Scottish	4,890,581	1.7	34	Japanese	1,103,325	0.4
12	Dutch	4,541,770	1.6	35	Cuban	1,097,594	0.4
13	Norwegian	4,477,725	1.6	36	British	1,085,718	0.4
14	Scotch-Irish	4,319,232	1.5	37	Vietnamese	1,029,420	0.4
15	Swedish	3,998,310	1.4	38	Swiss	911,502	0.3
16	White[1]	3,834,122	1.4	39	Dominican	908,531	0.3
17	Puerto Rican	2,652,598	0.9	40	Ukrainian	892,922	0.3
18	Russian	2,652,214	0.9	41	Salvadoran	802,743	0.3
19	Hispanic[1]	2,451,109	0.9	42	Slovak	797,764	0.3
20	French Canadian	2,349,684	0.8	43	Jamaican	736,513	0.3
21	Chinese	2,271,562	0.8	44	Austrian	730,336	0.3

(continued)

RANK	ANCESTRY	NUMBER	PERCENT
45	Lithuanian	659,992	0.2
46	Canadian	638,548	0.2
47	Finnish	623,559	0.2
48	Colombian	583,986	0.2
49	Haitian	548,199	0.2
50	Guatemalan	463,502	0.2
51	Czechoslovakian	441,403	0.2
52	Lebanese	440,279	0.2
53	Scandinavian	425,099	0.2
54	United States[1]	404,328	0.1
55	Armenian	385,488	0.1
56	Croatian	374,241	0.1
57	Romanian	367,278	0.1
58	Belgian	348,531	0.1
59	Iranian	338,266	0.1
60	Hawaiian	334,858	0.1
61	Yugoslavian	328,547	0.1
62	Ecuadorian	322,965	0.1
63	Spaniard	299,948	0.1
64	Taiwanese	293,568	0.1
65	Peruvian	292,991	0.1
66	Honduran	266,848	0.1
67	Pennsylvania German	255,807	0.1
68	Pakistani	253,193	0.1
69	Latin American[1]	250,052	0.1

RANK	ANCESTRY	NUMBER	PERCENT
70	Asian[1]	238,960	0.1
71	Nicaraguan	230,358	0.1
72	Arab[1]	205,822	0.1
73	Cambodian	197,093	0.1
74	Brazilian	181,076	0.1
75	Laotian	179,866	0.1
76	Slovene	176,691	0.1
77	Trinidadian and Tobagonian	164,738	0.1
78	Nigerian	164,691	0.1
79	Northern European[1]	163,657	0.1
80	Guyanese	162,425	0.1
81	West Indian[1]	147,222	0.1
82	Thai	146,577	0.1
83	Syrian	142,897	0.1
84	Egyptian	142,832	0.1
85	Hmong	140,528	—
86	Serbian	140,337	—
87	Slavic	127,136	—
88	Western European[1]	125,300	—
89	Panamanian	119,497	—
90	Turkish	117,575	—
91	Albanian	113,661	—
92	Israeli	106,839	—
	Other ancestries	4,380,380	1.6

Source: U.S. Census Bureau, Ancestry: 2000, issued June 2004.
[1]Groups may encompass several ancestries not listed separately.

FOUR

Native Americans

*Stereotypes are devices for saving a biased person the trouble
of learning.*

—ANONYMOUS

Our indigenous people—the real natives of our land—have been dis-
placed, treated as outlanders, and cheated more than just about any ethnic population in this nation's history. Today, perhaps more so than for
any other population group, the painful vestiges of the past linger on
for Native Americans, in the isolation and imagery that keep many in this
group on the outside looking in at the United States.

For generations, the public has been conditioned by educational institutions, the media, and the advertising and sports marketing worlds,
through the use of exaggerated and inaccurate labeling, to trivialize Native American culture.

As with most stereotyping, the pattern was established early. Falsified
or distorted stories set forth by America's colonizers slowly became universal "truths" to mainstream society. The practice cruelly reduced this
country's indigenous cultures to little more than cartoon caricatures in
the eyes of the so-called mainstream populace. To this day, vestiges of that

same movement remain, distorting history and impeding the path to self-determination for many Native Americans.

In the case of Native Americans, profit and fear were driving factors in the forming of public perception. Even today, the media and our history books are slow to own up to the broken treaties, recurring betrayals, seizures of land, and near-genocidal actions that were inflicted on this continent's native peoples over the course of more than five hundred years.

Laws were created that restricted language, intermarriage, and the religious and cultural practices of Native Americans. For example, in order to be granted land ownership or citizenship, Native Americans in the late 1700s had to formally renounce their "Indian-ness" and prove that they had adopted European lifestyles, manners, and values. They also had to provide church baptism records or evidence that they knew how to farm or had basic European-style homemaking skills. It was "be like us or suffer the consequences." Well into the late 1800s, formal education was required for all Native American children.

LABELS

There are many negative and positive terms to describe cultural groups, and each one can connote something a little different. But each illustrates the problem with all labels. They are limiting.

From the absurd Tonto characterizations on *The Lone Ranger* to the trite Land o' Lakes Indian Maiden image, Native Americans are one of the most mislabeled, misrepresented, and marginalized minorities in the history of the country. Accurate images of what the real modern-day Native population is like remain scarce. Few Native Americans can grow up without reading that their people were "savages" who interfered with the progress of Western civilization. In many historical contexts, they are cast as villains, if recognized at all.

Physically, Native Americans are commonly depicted one-dimensionally. Just as Europeans or African Americans do not all look alike, neither do Native Americans. Native Americans are also of many physical types and can have European, African, and other ancestry.

The term *Indian,* though still used in many places, is a slowly fading, somewhat ill-placed label in itself. It originated as a misnomer, based on the erroneous assumption that Christopher Columbus had landed in India when he first dropped anchor in the Bahamas in 1492. However, many tribes still bear the name "Indians," as do several Native American organizations. Use the word in its generic sense only with caution, however.

Such terms as *scalper, war whoop, squaw, red, red man, redskin, Injun,* and *papoose* should stay out of your lexicon. *Indian giver,* once in common use, is now patently offensive to Native Americans. The term *shaman* can also be offensive when applied to Native Americans. Teachers should avoid references and craft activities that trivialize Native American dress, dance, and beliefs. For example, the construction of paper headdresses for a Thanksgiving project can be offensive to some Native American students.

The terms *Native American, Natives, First Nations People,* and *Indigenous People* are more historically accurate and acceptable. Stereotypes and clichés such as *spiritual people* or *stoic people* may seem flattering to their unwitting users, but they are just one step above the "noble savage" image and are condescending in their implication that the population has few other attributes. Such language reduces Native Americans to exotic curios.

NEVER: *scalper, squaw, savage, red, red man, redskin, Injun, Indian giver*

BE CAREFUL WITH: *Indian, Spiritual People*

BEST: *Native American, First Nations People, Indigenous People*

Mascots, logos, and nicknames have also played a huge role in shaping mistaken portrayals of Native Americans. At junior high schools, high schools, and college campuses around the country, Native American students feel uncomfortable with the use of a stereotypical Indian as a school mascot to excite crowds at games. Many feel it is dishonorable, disrespectful, and confusing, especially to young Native Americans who are still struggling to form their senses of identity.

Despite continuing protests from Native Americans, pro sports teams such as the Washington Redskins, Atlanta Braves, Kansas City Chiefs, and Cleveland Indians continue to use absurdly clichéd mascots. Cleveland's "Chief Wahoo" logo and mascot, for example, offends many Native American people the same way that the racist tale of Little Black Sambo does African Americans, and the stereotypical, now-defunct TV advertising figure of the Frito Bandito offended the Hispanic community.

Many collegiate teams have joined a progressive movement nationwide to change the practice of co-opting Native American mascots and symbols for their teams. The St. John's Redmen recently became Redstorm, while the Stanford and Dartmouth Indians long ago changed their

Native American Timeline

1492	1540	1595 (approx.)
Christopher Columbus lands in the Bahamas and mistakenly identifies the island as India. The North American continent is home to 5 million Native Americans speaking as many as two thousand languages.	The Jesuit ministry begins securing a stronger foothold in both South and North America in its attempts to convert Native Americans to Christianity.	Pocahontas, daughter of Powhatan, and the most renowned Native American woman in American history, is born.

names to the Cardinals and Big Green, respectively. Since the early 1970s, more than two-thirds of the approximately three thousand plus colleges and schools that used such symbols have abandoned them.

The National Collegiate Athletic Association has recently taken a more serious look at the issue when it began considering whether it should stop scheduling championship events in states that fly the Confederate flag or assimilate it into their state flags. In August of 2005, the NCAA announced it would ban the use of Native American mascots and logos by sports teams in postseason NCAA tournaments starting in August of 2008—though not in the regular season or in major bowl games. The rule prohibits displays of "hostile or abusive" references on uniforms of teams, bands, and cheerleaders during the postseason tournaments.

The ban affects such school teams as the Southeastern Oklahoma State Savages, North Dakota Fighting Sioux, Bradley Braves, Illinois Illini, Carthage College Redmen and the teams of about a dozen other universities. Beginning in early 2006, institutions displaying hostile mascots or imagery could no longer host any type of NCAA championship competition.

A lawsuit aimed at stripping the Washington NFL franchise of its

1621

Massasoit, chief of the Wampanoag tribe, signs a peace treaty with the Pilgrims on March 22. The Algonquian Samoset cedes twelve thousand acres to the new arrivals. The first Thanksgiving occurs.

1673

With the aid of a Native guide, Joliet and Marquette chart the Mississippi River as far south as the Arkansas River.

1711–13

Settlers begin encroaching on farmland of the Tuscaroras, who have previously maintained friendly relations with the colonists in an area of North Carolina. The settlers begin to cheat them in trades and in some cases kidnap and sell their children into slavery. The Tuscaroras, who are related to the Iroquois, retaliate by raiding white villages in 1711. An retaliatory army raid kills or captures one thousand Natives.

Redskins trademark on the grounds that it violates federal law by disparaging Native Americans has been considered, as were bills in California and Oklahoma that would outlaw the use of such nicknames and mascots in public schools.

AN INVISIBLE RACE?

Unfortunately, the unique type of social and economic disconnect suffered by Native Americans since the birth of our nation makes the group's culture much more likely to accept social labels and problems as a way of life. It doesn't take a leap in logic to trace increasing substance abuse, gang problems, and other destructive self-actualizing experiences to the negative portrayal and marginalization of Native Americans in our culture and the resulting mind-numbing impact on self-image.

In fact, a Children Now study indicates that Native American children practically think of themselves as an invisible race in the media. "Yet, when they do see themselves, they're often troubled by what they see," said the organization's president, Lois Salisbury. The scarcity of Native Americans on television, combined with "their portrayal as poor, drunk, living on reservations, selling fireworks, and fighting over land," only per-

1754–63

The French and Indian War, the culmination of French efforts to drive British fur traders out of the Ohio Valley, is waged. The Cherokee generally side with the British in the war, but a dispute in 1760 over a group of wild horses prompts the English to kill numerous Cherokee, inciting a raid on British settlements. Britain retaliates with a "scorched earth" policy. The war ends with the Treaty of Paris, which gives large tracts of Algonquian land to Britain. Pontiac, heading a league of eighteen Algonquian-speaking tribes, begins a campaign against the British. The Proclamation of 1763 separates Indian land from European settlements.

1803

The United States purchases the Louisiana Territory from France. The ensuing westward expansion leads to the depletion of buffalo.

petuates stereotypes and contributes to low self-esteem among their children, the study concluded.

Though learning and teaching have always been high on the Native American priority list, only 50 percent of this group will get their high school diploma, and just 17 percent will attempt college (National Science Foundation, 2000). There are many cultural and socioeconomic reasons for this record, including life on remotely located reservations, a shortage of Native American role models, language differences, and low income levels. But a general suspicion of the traditional American education system also remains strong—and for good reason.

Well through the middle of the twentieth century, school policies regularly forbade Native languages, banned traditional practices, burned Native children's clothing, and cut their hair. Native American students were relocated to poorly maintained, often disease-ridden boarding schools that were usually at great distances from their families.

As a result, more than two generations of Native Americans all but lost their identities in the American education system. Sitting Bull, a prominent leader in the Sioux resistance to white encroachment in the mineral-rich Black Hills of South Dakota, was once quoted as saying, "Let us put our minds together and see what kind of life we can make for

1804	1811–14	1818
Sacagawea, a Shoshone captured as a child by Minnetaree Natives and later sold to Toussaint Charbonneau, marries Charbonneau. They jointly lead the Lewis and Clark Expedition as guides.	William Henry Harrison takes a militia of a thousand men and marches on the Native settlement of Prophetstown, founded by Tecumseh. Meanwhile, settlers are impatient to claim Native lands in Georgia, and the Creek tribe sees its territories diminish. An estimated 750 Creek die in the Battle of Horseshoe Bend. General Andrew Jackson then sets up camp in the heart of Creek country, and many Creek leaders come forward to surrender.	General Andrew Jackson defeats a force of Native Americans and African Americans to end the First Seminole War.

our children." But today Native Americans still suffer from isolation in America's school systems.

In all, it is estimated that North America was once home to 5 million Native Americans, who spoke between one and two thousand different languages (Washburn, 1975; Driver, 1961) when Columbus arrived in 1492. Today, there are only eight groupings for the remaining Native American languages, including Iroquoian, Muskogean, Caddoan, and Athapaskan.

Native American children who look to contemporary culture for positive Native American role models needn't come up empty. However, author Terri Jean, organizer of the Red Roots Educational Project and editor of *The Native Truth,* said she recently polled about forty young children ages four to twelve and asked them to name five famous Native Americans. Most knew great historical figures such as Sitting Bull, Crazy Horse, and Tecumseh. But when asked to name contemporary Natives, only a handful could answer, and they could only identify one, Wilma Mankiller, the first female principal chief of the Cherokee Nation of Oklahoma. Many attribute this ignorance to the fact that fewer than 15 percent of teachers of Native American students are themselves Native American and cannot adequately or accurately reflect Native

1825	1830	1831–32
The Treaty of Indian Springs gives large tracts of ancestral land to Georgia.	The Indian Removal Act requires the removal of Native Americans from east of the Mississippi River to a newly established Indian Territory in what is now Oklahoma. Tribes removed included the Shawnee, Potawatomis, Kickapoo, and Winnebago.	The Supreme Court upholds the right of the Cherokee to remain on their lands. Despite that, President Andrew Jackson sends federal troops to forcibly remove the Cherokee and other tribes. The Cherokee are removed during harsh winter conditions, causing hardship and loss of life, in a time tribes remember as the Trail of Tears.

American culture and history, according to the World's Indigenous Women's Foundation.

LEADERS

Though Native Americans have often been thwarted in their attempts to retain their unique culture and heritage, it hasn't been for want of leaders. The following Native Americans took crucial first steps toward transcending—moving past the constraints that others imposed on them.

Jim Thorpe

One of the twentieth century's widely acknowledged early Native American role models was James Francis Thorpe, who was born in a one-room cabin in Oklahoma on May 28, 1887. A Native American of Sac and Fox heritage, Thorpe managed to rise high from his humble origins and the social stigmas of the times thanks to his extraordinary talent and determination. His Native name, Wa-Tho-Huk, translates appropriately as "Bright Path." And a searing trail Thorpe did blaze.

To this day, ninety-four years after his astounding performance at the 1912 Olympic Games, Thorpe is still considered one of the greatest ath-

1835–42	1848	1851
Jackson tries to move the Seminoles out of Florida, leading to the second war between the tribe and United States. Seminoles refuse to cede their land; they give refuge to runaway slaves. Slave owners demand immediate retribution. The army commits atrocities, including hunting Natives with bloodhounds.	The Gold Rush in California results in a drop in the California Native American population from 120,000 in 1850 to fewer than 20,000 by 1880. Natives, no longer able because of environmental changes to pursue their traditional means of procuring food, raid mining camps for food.	The governor of California condones a policy of extermination against California Indians.

letes of all time. He won both the pentathlon and decathlon events that year and set several performance and point-total records in the process, prompting King Gustav V of Sweden to tell him, "Sir, you are the greatest athlete in the world." No one would surpass his decathlon score for fifteen years.

The same year, Thorpe led his Carlisle Indian School football squad to the national collegiate championship, scoring twenty-five touchdowns and 198 points. But a year later, Thorpe was stripped of his Olympic medals and records when it was discovered that he had played semipro baseball for a few dollars—a common practice for struggling student athletes of the day.

But the Amateur Athletic Union (AAU) of America chose to make an example of him, claiming Thorpe was not a true amateur, and stripped him of his medals and records. So Thorpe departed Carlisle and played major and minor league baseball for ten seasons and football in the National Football League until 1929, when he retired at forty-one—an ancient age for an athlete of that era.

In the process, Thorpe helped change the face of pro football from the old American Professional Football Association into the more solvent NFL in 1922, and he even became its first league president. Thorpe's

1861	1867	1868
Some tribes, including the so-called Five Civilized Tribes of the Southeast, side with the Confederacy in the Civil War in exchange for promises of respect for Indian sovereignty. After the war, the U.S. government punishes the Five Civilized Tribes by forcing them to cede land.	The largest treaty gathering in American history, between the United States and the Cheyenne and Arapaho Nations, results in the Treaty of Medicine Lodge. The two tribes are removed to a reservation created out of lands taken from the Five Civilized Tribes.	The U.S. Army, led by George Armstrong Custer, slaughters an unarmed gathering of Cheyenne, killing mostly women and children.

drive, renown, and credibility helped sow the seeds that have made the NFL the country's favorite sport today. Thorpe was voted "Athlete of the First Half of the Twentieth Century" in 1953.

Righting a wrong, the International Olympic Committee (IOC) restored his Olympic records and presented facsimile medals to his children in 1983—thirty years after Jim Thorpe died penniless. As the last century wound down, Thorpe was named ABC's *Wide World of Sports* Athlete of the Century.

Wilma Mankiller

At first, Wilma Mankiller's candidacy for the role of principal chief of the Cherokee Nation was opposed by those who did not want to be led by a woman. Death threats abounded, and her tires were slashed during her campaign. But she prevailed. With an enrolled population of more than 140,000, an annual budget exceeding $75 million, and more than 1,200 employees spread throughout 7,000 square miles, her role as head of the Cherokee was akin to that of a major corporate CEO.

As a child, Mankiller was moved to California with her family as part of the Bureau of Indian Affairs relocation program, which she detailed richly in her book, *Mankiller: A Chief and Her People*. When AIM (the

1874	1876	1881
An expedition led by Custer discovers gold in the Black Hills, sending a flood of prospectors to the region. The Sioux revolt.	Custer attacks a hunting camp of Sioux, Arapaho, and Cheyenne on the Little Big Horn River in Montana. Sitting Bull, Gall, Crazy Horse, and Cheyenne leaders defeat Custer and the Seventh Cavalry. Custer and 250 soldiers die in the famous battle.	Helen Hunt Jackson's *A Century of Dishonor*, which details the plight of Native Americans, is published.

American Indian Movement) occupied Alcatraz Island in 1969 with the goal of reclaiming federal land in the name of Native nations and attracting attention to tribal issues, Mankiller stood front and center in its support.

Mankiller would later go on to earn national recognition as a Native American activist and an expert in community development, although she suffered physically, often in great pain. After narrowly avoiding the amputation of her right leg in an accident in 1979, she endured seventeen operations. Mankiller was later diagnosed with myasthenia gravis, a neuromuscular disease that causes chronic weakness in the voluntary muscles of the body.

Billy Mills

Another Native American Olympian, Billy Mills, became a hero to the world for his triumphs and determination. Mills pulled off one of the most stunning upsets in the history of the games when he won the gold medal in the 10,000 meter race in the 1964 Tokyo Olympic Games. His Olympic record of 28 minutes, 24.4 seconds remains a great source of pride to Native Americans.

Mills, an Oglala Lakota who was born on the Pine Ridge Indian

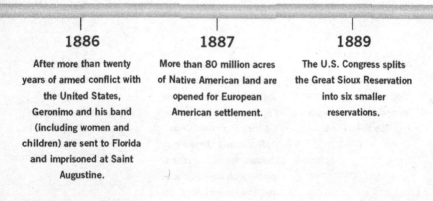

1886

After more than twenty years of armed conflict with the United States, Geronimo and his band (including women and children) are sent to Florida and imprisoned at Saint Augustine.

1887

More than 80 million acres of Native American land are opened for European American settlement.

1889

The U.S. Congress splits the Great Sioux Reservation into six smaller reservations.

Reservation in South Dakota, was orphaned at the age of twelve. He chose running as the positive focus in his life. The movie *Running Brave* is based on his life story.

Today Mills serves as national spokesperson for Running Strong for American Indian Youth, encouraging Native American youth with his positive messages of character, pride, and dignity. "Your life is a gift from the Creator," he has said. "Your gift back to the Creator is what you do with your life."

Though his father died when Mills was an adolescent, Mills remains motivated by his teachings: "I was constantly told and challenged to live my life as a warrior," he's been quoted as saying. "As a warrior, you assume responsibility for yourself. The warrior humbles himself. And the warrior learns the power of giving."

Mills wrote *Wokini: A Lakota Journey to Happiness and Understanding* with Nicholas Sparks; it is now in its eighth printing worldwide. Today Billy travels throughout the country speaking about "global unity through global diversity" to Native American communities, colleges, and corporations and acting as a mentor and role model for young Native Americans.

1890	1890s	1904
The Massacre at Wounded Knee Creek occurs. Armed troops open fire on a band of Big Lakota Sioux, killing 250 men, women, and children in an event often described as the last major conflict between the U.S. Army and the Sioux Nation.	The U.S. government begins a campaign to "civilize" Native Americans by rounding up Native American children and sending them to boarding schools. The children's hair is cut, their clothes are burned and replaced with European American dress, and they are forbidden to speak their native language.	Geronimo is exhibited along with other Native peoples at the Saint Louis World's Fair.

Winona LaDuke

Several other contemporary Native American leaders and role models continue to assert themselves as agents of change.

Environmentalist Winona LaDuke gained nationwide recognition as vice presidential running mate to Ralph Nader on the 1996 and 2000 Green Party tickets. The daughter of an Anishinabe father and a Jewish mother, LaDuke earned a degree in economic development from Harvard and later founded the White Earth Land Recovery Project, which works to buy back tribal lands. She also authored the novel *Last Standing Woman* and the history *All Our Relations: Native Struggles for Land and Life*.

LaDuke, a mother of three, was also founder of the Honor the Earth Fund and the Indigenous Women's Network, and she was named Woman of the Year by *Ms.* magazine in 1997. She appeared as an actor in the award-winning 2002 film *Skins*, which depicted the problems of alcoholism, unemployment, and domestic violence on the Pine Ridge Indian Reservation through the eyes of two Lakota Sioux Native American brothers.

1924

The Citizenship Act is passed, declaring all Native Americans U.S. citizens and entitling them to vote in national elections. An eight-hundred-page study financed by John D. Rockefeller finds Native Americans living in conditions of stark poverty and ill health.

1925

Native American suffrage is granted by act of Congress.

1934

The Indian Reorganization Act encourages Native Americans to recover their cultural heritage, restructures government Indian schools, and increases their funding with a condition that tribes adopt a U.S.-style constitution. Many tribes, including the Navajo, refuse. Native American children are allowed to attend schools closer to home, and reservation day schools are funded to teach tribal languages.

More Notables

John Herrington of the Chickasaw Nation was the first Native American to walk in space. Boarding the Space Shuttle *Endeavor,* launched in November 2002, he honored his heritage by carrying with him the Chickasaw Nation flag, six eagle feathers, a braid of sweetgrass, and two arrowheads. Members of his tribe watched the historic flight.

The multitalented Sherman Alexie, a poet, novelist, film producer, and screenwriter, produced in 1998 the award-winning movie *Smoke Signals,* the first U.S.-distributed feature film to be written, produced, acted, and directed by Native Americans. Alexie has also published the novels *Reservation Blues* and *Indian Killer* (the latter of which was named a *New York Times* Notable Book), seven books of poetry, a short-story collection called *The Lone Ranger and Tonto Fistfight in Heaven* and many other works.

Contemporary sports figures include figure skater Naomi Lang of California's Karuk Tribe. Partnering with Russian-born Peter Tchernyshev, Lang is the first Native American to participate in the Winter Olympics. The two are the 1999, 2000, 2001, 2002, and 2003 U.S. Ice Dance champions.

1950s	1968	1969
A "termination policy" is adopted, settling federal obligations to tribes, withdrawing federal support for Native American health services, education, and other programs, and closing many reservations. Tribal members are relocated to urban areas. Congress eventually terminates services to more than sixty tribes, including Klamaths, Paiutes, Menominees, Poncas, and Catawbas.	The American Indian Movement (AIM), rights group committed to uniting Native Peoples, is founded in Minneapolis with the mission of uplifting communities and promoting cultural pride and sovereignty.	A group of Native Americans, calling themselves "Indians of All Tribes," occupy Alcatraz Island in San Francisco Bay to protest conditions. The occupation will last two years and bring national attention to the problems faced by Native Americans.

Pro golfer Notah Begay, of Navajo, San Felipe, and Isleta heritage, joined the tough-to-crack PGA tour in 1999. Begay, a former collegiate teammate of Tiger Woods, has frequently said that more Native American athletes would emerge with stronger support networks and facilities.

Another notable Native American is actor, rapper, and entrepreneur Litefoot, of the Cherokee Nation. He released the cutting-edge album *The Money* on his own Red Vinyl Records in 1992 and vaulted to stardom, winning the Native American Music Award in 1996, 1998, and 1999. He also starred in the film *The Indian in the Cupboard* in 1995 and appeared in *Kull the Conqueror, Mortal Kombat: Annihilation,* and *Adaptation.*

ROOM FOR ECONOMIC ADVANCEMENT

While the role of Native Americans in American culture has improved somewhat, there's still ample room for economic advancement and a particular need for improved health care.

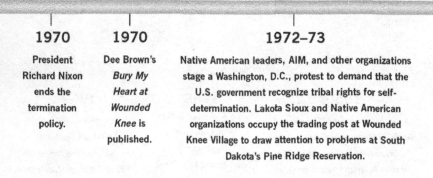

1970

President Richard Nixon ends the termination policy.

1970

Dee Brown's *Bury My Heart at Wounded Knee* is published.

1972–73

Native American leaders, AIM, and other organizations stage a Washington, D.C., protest to demand that the U.S. government recognize tribal rights for self-determination. Lakota Sioux and Native American organizations occupy the trading post at Wounded Knee Village to draw attention to problems at South Dakota's Pine Ridge Reservation.

Recent census data show that more than 30 percent of the Native American population live below the poverty line, versus roughly 13 percent for all races. Many of the impoverished are children living in rural and frontier areas, where health services are difficult to reach or are outdated, and where safe and adequate water supplies and waste-disposal facilities are less common than in the U.S. general population. Health-care providers, while doing their best to provide quality care, say they are underfunded and understaffed and overwhelmed by need.

The Native American infant mortality rate is still 22 percent higher than that of the general population and 60 percent higher than the rate for whites, according to the American Academy of Pediatrics. Suicide rates are twice as high among five- to fourteen-year-olds. Alcohol-related deaths among Native American ages fifteen to twenty-four are seventeen times higher than the national average. The population remains twice as likely as other Americans in general to die through the age of twenty-four.

These sad statistics are related to the extreme poverty of the popula-

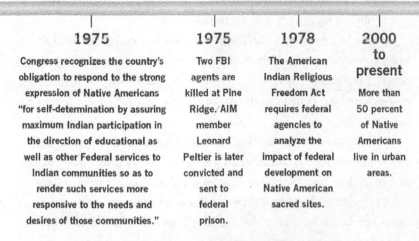

1975	1975	1978	2000 to present
Congress recognizes the country's obligation to respond to the strong expression of Native Americans "for self-determination by assuring maximum Indian participation in the direction of educational as well as other Federal services to Indian communities so as to render such services more responsive to the needs and desires of those communities."	Two FBI agents are killed at Pine Ridge. AIM member Leonard Peltier is later convicted and sent to federal prison.	The American Indian Religious Freedom Act requires federal agencies to analyze the impact of federal development on Native American sacred sites.	More than 50 percent of Native Americans live in urban areas.

Sources: Legends of America.com; www.infoplease.com; Stephen Trimble, The People: Indians of the American Southwest, *Santa Fe School of American Research Press, 1993; James Olson and Raymond Wilson,* Native Americans in the Twentieth Century, *University of Illinois Press, 1986.*

tion. Other health disparities, such as high rates of diabetes and injury morbidity and excessive mortality rates, prevail as well. Unfortunately, countless Native Americans have fallen through cracks in the health-care system. Many Natives say the bureaucracy and myriad rules involved in the delivery of the health care promised to them in treaties is so burdensome that many in the population simply forgo Medicare and Medicaid enrollment and care.

Economically, the relatively swift spread of Native American gaming in the past few decades has brought economic independence and better health care to thousands, although some studies show that proceeds benefit a relative few, excluding the poor.

Many Native tribes are turning their newfound earnings into influence by amplifying lobby efforts and contributing millions of dollars to political campaigns. Hence, while Native Americans constitute only 1 percent of the electorate, they now have a stronger political voice in the form of a fatter wallet and, until recently, a legislator. Colorado's U.S. Senator Ben Nighthorse Campbell, who became the first Native American to serve in the Senate in more than sixty years upon his election in 1992, served two terms but did not run for a third, although he hinted at a possible run for governor in the future.

Native Americans are also increasing their buying power, from $42.5 billion in 2003 to a projected $65.1 billion in 2008, according to the Selig Center at the University of Georgia. Native Americans account for an estimated 0.6 percent of the nation's buying power, up from 0.5 percent in 1990.

Even with economic and political advances, threats to Native American tribal sovereignty continue to appear in many forms, from federal and state challenges to the authority of tribal courts to new taxation.

But perhaps the biggest threat of all comes from society's continuing characterizations of Native Americans as "noble savages" and other demeaning stereotypes. The biggest challenge in how we view Native Americans may be to abandon those old "Indian of the Mind" notions to see the real Native Americans standing at our sides. It is a process in which we can all participate.

When you transcend the labels and stereotypes of others, you see the real person before you. Once accomplished, that victory will help the other person see the real you. The blinders you may not have realized you've been wearing simply fall off, and you may both realize that you have transformed without having to shed your skin.

Discussion Questions

1. Who benefited from the early characterizations of Native Americans?

2. How did some Native American leaders rise above their labels?

3. How do the current struggles of the Native American population relate to old labels and stereotypes?

4. What does it mean to be Native American today?

FIVE

Latinos and Hispanic Americans

Great spirits have always found violent opposition from medi-
ocrities. The latter cannot understand it when a man does not
thoughtlessly submit to hereditary prejudices but honestly and
courageously uses his intelligence.

—*ALBERT EINSTEIN*

It's official. Latinos/Hispanics are now the largest minority in America. In
fact, the Census Bureau estimates that by the year 2050, Latinos will
make up roughly one-fourth of the U.S. population, and by 2100, they'll
represent a third.

In the big picture, a vigorous, diverse, and influential Latino population will continue to emerge with those dynamic growth projections. But
at present, the population's future continues to be undermined by a sub-
standard educational and socioeconomic standing, whose roots lie partially in slow-to-die stereotypes and labels.

Today Latinos remain typecast as laborers and migrants at a time
when the U.S. system seems content with perpetuating that image. Much

as with other minority populations, the positive portrayal of Hispanics in the English-speaking broadcast media is still relatively uncommon. Latinos playing TV and movie roles as successful doctors, lawyers, or other educated professionals are rare. Instead, Hispanics are often depicted as illegal immigrants, criminals, and exaggerated comedic figures who speak in broken English.

Remember, it wasn't long ago that the Taco Bell dog was perpetuating antiquated stereotypes daily on TV, in the tradition of the insulting Frito Bandito figure. (Around 1970, one watch manufacturer ran a newspaper ad portraying one of the heroes of the Mexican Revolution, Emiliano Zapata, as a thief willing to kill for watches!) The Spanish-speaking media also come up short in the depiction of positive, nonstereotypical Hispanic role models, say Latino journalists and business leaders.

Studies have shown that nearly two-thirds of Latinos don't feel that television represents them accurately. In 1999, Hispanic groups such as the National Council of La Raza (NCLA) joined with the NAACP in protesting the lack of minority roles in prime-time shows in the fall lineup. The groups urged viewers to participate in a national brownout of

Latino and Hispanic American Timeline

1492–93	1513	1521	1565
Spaniards land on the island of San Salvador in the eastern Bahamas. Columbus lands on the northeastern coast. On a second voyage, Columbus discovers Puerto Rico and the Virgin Islands.	Ponce de León lands, explores the coastal regions and portions of the interior of Florida. An estimated 100,000 Native Americans lived in Florida at the time.	Cortés and his Spanish contingent destroy the Aztec city of Tenochtitlán and begin building Mexico City on the ruins.	The earliest North America settlement is founded in Saint Augustine, Florida. Until 1819, Saint Augustine is a Spanish possession.

the ABC, CBS, NBC, and Fox networks the week of September 12 to co-incide with Hispanic Heritage Week. The networks all responded by hiring numerous minority actors for additional roles in their fall shows. Some vestiges of those actions remain.

Today we see a great deal of economic hypocrisy in the employment of migrant workers or undocumented workers from Mexico. Some criss-cross the border illegally to improve the lives of their families. Some intend to return to Mexico, while others hope to remain in the United States and eventually become citizens. But what they have in common is a desperate desire to succeed and to belong. They aspire for a dream that has brought so many immigrants of all lands to the United States.

It's doubtful that those who are risking their lives have sinister or imperialist motives when they are enduring terrible conditions just for the chance to live a better life. They're no doubt living day to day, without thoughts of stealing jobs from Americans or defiantly speaking Spanish instead of learning English. Economically, they provide a needed service, and many employers know they can get away with paying them less than they would a legal resident. Because these workers lack legal status and representation, some simply accept their exploitation. Business owners also know that they are paying these workers more than they would make

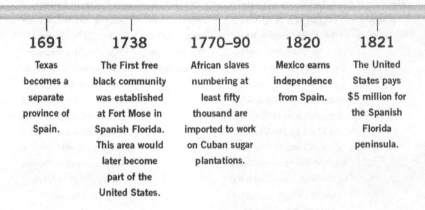

1691	1738	1770–90	1820	1821
Texas becomes a separate province of Spain.	The First free black community was established at Fort Mose in Spanish Florida. This area would later become part of the United States.	African slaves numbering at least fifty thousand are imported to work on Cuban sugar plantations.	Mexico earns independence from Spain.	The United States pays $5 million for the Spanish Florida peninsula.

in Mexico and that the workers will not question their business practices because of residency issues. This scenario continues to make business owners wealthier. They are able to offer cheap wages without benefits, yet have all their labor needs met. The vulnerable undocumented workers have no choice but to accept these terms, and the trend continues.

Many of these workforce issues came into focus in the spring of 2006 when tens of thousands of Hispanics and immigration advocates took to the streets of American cities to demand that Congress abandon its attempts to build walls along the U.S.-Mexican border while making illegal immigration a felony. Chanting *"Sí, se puede,"* an old Mexican American civil rights slogan meaning "Yes, we can," the peaceful demonstrators grabbed the attention of the world in one of the largest exhibitions of Hispanic clout in the history of America. They pulled back the curtain on the economic and social impacts of the issue, spurring a more balanced and open debate on the sensitive subject.

1829

Slavery is abolished in Mexico.

1836

Anglo-Texans resist the military rule of Antonio López de Santa Anna, dictator of Mexico. Led by Santa Anna, an army heads to San Antonio and surrounds the Texans at the Alamo mission. The resisters are killed by the Mexican army. Six weeks later the Mexican forces are defeated by the Anglo-Texans and the Republic of Texas becomes independent of Mexico.

1845

The United States annexes Texas, angering the Mexican government.

1846

The United States invades Mexico under the banner of Manifest Destiny. The Treaty of Guadalupe Hidalgo ends the Mexican War. As a result, the United States gains half the land area of Mexico, including Texas, California, most of Arizona and New Mexico, and parts of Colorado, Utah, and Nevada.

LABELS AND DISCRIMINATION

Stereotypes and labels often act like codes, whether they relate to women, class, race, jobs, or sexual orientation. They give observers a quick, capsulated view of a person or group of people that is often tantamount to negative reinforcement. Their users often amuse one another with them. That is programming that can be tough to purge. Studies have shown that no matter how committed we are to evenhandedness or how hard we work to act without prejudice, we still possess hidden negative stereotypes and prejudices that may influence our actions and perceptions. That's why it's essential to make a consistent effort to see past these generalizations, which are particularly prevalent in depictions of the Latino community. Too often, Latino adults are seen as only the helping class, serving as hired hands, scrubbing floors and trimming shrubs.

As insidious as the many slurs attached to this population are the more subtle labels and false perceptions of Latinos, including the notion that they're all "foreign" because they may have Spanish surnames. That

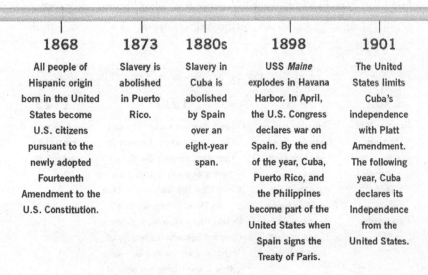

1868	1873	1880s	1898	1901
All people of Hispanic origin born in the United States become U.S. citizens pursuant to the newly adopted Fourteenth Amendment to the U.S. Constitution.	Slavery is abolished in Puerto Rico.	Slavery in Cuba is abolished by Spain over an eight-year span.	USS *Maine* explodes in Havana Harbor. In April, the U.S. Congress declares war on Spain. By the end of the year, Cuba, Puerto Rico, and the Philippines become part of the United States when Spain signs the Treaty of Paris.	The United States limits Cuba's independence with Platt Amendment. The following year, Cuba declares its Independence from the United States.

sentiment prevails despite the reality that hundreds of places throughout the United States have had names of Spanish origin for a couple of hundred years, and that many American Hispanic families date back ten generations or more.

The truth is, Hispanics are quite unlike any previous groups of immigrants, because many aren't immigrants at all. The Hispanic population has been here in North America for more than 450 years and has legitimately established Spanish as a second language in the United States alongside English.

But when people are uniformly dubbed foreigners, erroneous assumptions follow. One is that their population has had little or no stake in the American system, an assumption that diminishes the roles they have—and have long had—in building our country. People often assume Latinos either don't speak English or learned it only recently. Of course, many have never spoken anything *but* English. Such assumptions also imply that Hispanics aren't suited for white-collar or professional jobs.

It took a *20/20* broadcast—"The Name Game: Can Your Name Hold You Back in a Job Search?"—to confirm what Latinos and people of various ethnic groups have suspected for years. The more ethnic-

1902	1910	1917	1925
Thousands of Hispanic Americans lose their land under the Reclamation Act.	Hundreds of thousands flee to the north from Mexico as the Mexican Revolution begins. Many remain in the southwest United States.	Mexican miners and farm and railroad laborers are temporarily permitted to enter the United States as workers during the World War. The Jones Act, which grants U.S. citizenship to all Puerto Rican citizens, is passed. Two publicly elected houses of legislature are created in Puerto Rico. English becomes official language of Puerto Rico.	Congress creates the Border Patrol.

sounding the name, the less attention from employers an applicant stands to get in many situations. A young man writing on UrbanInsider.com lamented the fact that he'd sent out as many as a thousand résumés with no success until he hired a human resources consultant. The consultant suggested he change his application name from Miguel to Mike. He did and got seven interviews within a month, shortly landing a well-paying job as a chemical engineer.

Another stereotype assumes that Hispanic populations are mostly a regional phenomenon, centered in southern, southwestern, and western states bordering Mexico. Chicago, with 750,000 Hispanics, alone refutes that notion. In fact, it is the third-largest Hispanic city in the country. The problem with such thinking is that it is provincial: it fails to view Latino citizens as a national presence, regarding them as merely a local issue instead of the important national phenomenon they are.

Despite making strides, much of this population continues to miss out the American dream. The median net worth of Hispanic households in 2002 was just $7,932, or 9 percent of the $88,651 median wealth of non-Hispanic white households (Pew Hispanic Center, "The Wealth of Hispanic Households: 1996 to 2002"). The net worth of non-Hispanic African American households stood at only $5,988 in 2002, meaning

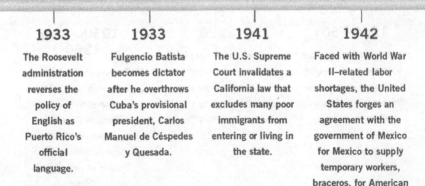

1933	1933	1941	1942
The Roosevelt administration reverses the policy of English as Puerto Rico's official language.	Fulgencio Batista becomes dictator after he overthrows Cuba's provisional president, Carlos Manuel de Céspedes y Quesada.	The U.S. Supreme Court invalidates a California law that excludes many poor immigrants from entering or living in the state.	Faced with World War II–related labor shortages, the United States forges an agreement with the government of Mexico for Mexico to supply temporary workers, braceros, for American farm work.

that the combined median wealth of Latino and African American households was *less than a tenth* of the wealth of the average white household.

The media continue to present errant perceptions of the U.S. Latino population, which in size is led by Mexican Americans (63 percent) and Puerto Rican Americans (10 percent). An independent media study performed by Indiana University professor David Weaver and his colleagues suggests that in the newsroom itself, minority representation is proceeding at a dawdling pace. In 1992, 8.2 percent of America's journalists were people of color. That proportion increased only to 9.5 percent by 2002. If that rate holds, only 16 percent of America's journalists will be people of color by 2050 in a country where more than 50 percent of the news consumers will be. The president of the National Association of Hispanic Journalists, New York *Daily News* columnist Juan Gonzales, observed that newsrooms "obviously aren't going to be anywhere near the population's diversity unless nationwide, new strategies are developed by some of these [media] companies."

There's no question that the many strong adult role models in the Hispanic population need to be elevated to the mainstream, not only to change false perceptions but to help reduce shocking school dropout rates among Latino teens. While Hispanics represent the country's fastest-

1940s–50s	1950	1950s–early 1960s
Hispanic workers and union advocates push for labor reform as unionization increases rapidly among Hispanic workers.	Puerto Rico's political status is upgraded from protectorate to commonwealth by the U.S. Congress.	Segregation in Arizona, Texas, and other states is abolished thanks to the efforts of the Alianza Hispano Americana organizations and the League of United Latin American Citizens (LULAC).

growing ethnic population, only about 11 percent of the population completes four years of college. As Latino leaders point out, both the media and the educational system need to help Hispanic youth see that people who look like them have succeeded by completing high school and pursuing higher education and professional careers—and not just by becoming entertainers. Too often, Latino children see adults depicted only as the helping class, servants and hired hands.

That's why it is so important that successful businesspeople, academics, graduate students, or anyone who's benefited from a higher education should volunteer to speak to elementary, junior high, and high school Latino students. Similarly, corporations should encourage their Latino employees to reach out to students and tell their success stories in order to help nurture the next generation of talented people. A transformation in this mind-set can be facilitated if more Hispanic leaders reach out to their communities to display the diversity of their talents and strengths.

Some of the most overtly offensive labels are words such as *beaner, greaser, meskin, taco bender, wetback, peon,* and the like. But using names such as *Paco, Chico,* and *Pancho* to describe Latinos in a generic sense can be offensive as well, even though some in the Hispanic population have those names.

1954	1954–58	1959
In a Supreme Court case briefed and argued by Mexican American lawyers, the Court recognizes that Hispanics have suffered systemic discrimination, clearing the way for Hispanic Americans to attack discrimination in U.S. courts.	A government effort to locate and deport undocumented workers called Operation Wetback results in massive deportations, though only a small number of those deported get deportation hearings. Thousands of others of Mexican descent are detained or arrested.	Fidel Castro and his followers overthrow Batista in the Cuban Revolution, leading to massive migration of Cubans to the United States.

Low rider is another such thinly veiled derogatory term, while referring to Latinos as "hot-blooded" can also be derisive. *FOB*, short for "fresh over the border," has crept into the lexicon of American slurs. Use *Latino* or *Hispanic*, or reference a country of origin with such terms as *Mexican American, Spanish American*, or *Cuban American.*

NEVER: *beaner, greaser, meskin, wetback, low rider, FOB*

BE CAREFUL WITH: *names such as* Paco *and* Pancho *used to describe Hispanics generically, the word* Chicano

BEST: *Latino, Hispanic, or a term denoting specific ethnicity: Mexican American, Spanish American,*

LEADERS

Antonio Villaraigosa

Successful Latino American role models continue to grow in number and influence. One is Los Angeles mayor Antonio Villaraigosa. He grew up a Chicano child in impoverished East Los Angeles, raised by a single

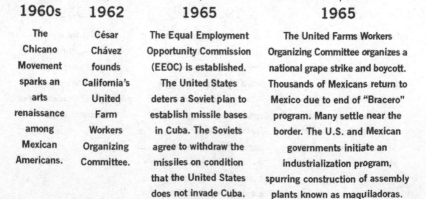

1960s	1962	1965	1965
The Chicano Movement sparks an arts renaissance among Mexican Americans.	César Chávez founds California's United Farm Workers Organizing Committee.	The Equal Employment Opportunity Commission (EEOC) is established. The United States deters a Soviet plan to establish missile bases in Cuba. The Soviets agree to withdraw the missiles on condition that the United States does not invade Cuba.	The United Farms Workers Organizing Committee organizes a national grape strike and boycott. Thousands of Mexicans return to Mexico due to end of "Bracero" program. Many settle near the border. The U.S. and Mexican governments initiate an industrialization program, spurring construction of assembly plants known as maquiladoras.

mother. At age seven, he would take a bus downtown to sell newspapers and shine shoes. In tenth grade, he was diagnosed with a tumor that partially paralyzed his legs. But he recovered and received enough encouragement from a couple of kind and conscientious teachers not only to graduate from high school but to go on to UCLA and eventually to law school. With his decisive May 2005 election victory, he became the first candidate to oust a sitting mayor of Los Angeles in thirty-two years.

Villaraigosa joins a growing list of influential Latino politicians, a group that includes Senator Ken Salazar of Colorado, Representative Robert Menendez of New Jersey, Florida representative Ileana Ros-Lehtinen (the first Cuban American in Congress), Oklahoma governor Bill Richardson, and Representative Henry Bonilla of Texas.

Ann Marie Tallman

Ann Marie Tallman, a granddaughter of Mexican migrant workers, also exemplifies Hispanic leadership. Tallman has worked tirelessly to become one of the most influential women in the U.S. financial services industry and to serve as a voice for Latinos and non-Latinos alike.

The first in her family to attend college, Tallman graduated with honors from the University of Iowa with degrees in psychology and political

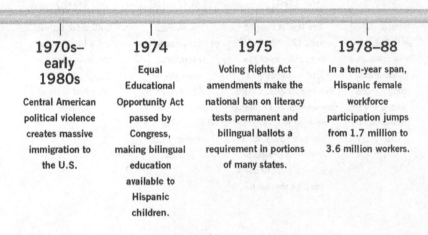

1970s–early 1980s	1974	1975	1978–88
Central American political violence creates massive immigration to the U.S.	Equal Educational Opportunity Act passed by Congress, making bilingual education available to Hispanic children.	Voting Rights Act amendments make the national ban on literacy tests permanent and bilingual ballots a requirement in portions of many states.	In a ten-year span, Hispanic female workforce participation jumps from 1.7 million to 3.6 million workers.

science before earning her law degree from UC Berkeley. Along the way, she worked full-time in the cornfields, in kitchens, and in other less-than-comfortable places to help support her family and earn her way through school. Professionally, Tallman soon progressed from deputy director of planning and community development for both the city and county of Denver to later serve a full decade in major executive posts with mortgage financing giant Fannie Mae.

As president and CEO of the nonprofit Fannie Mae Foundation in Washington, D.C., she reengineered the organization while also launching the Hispanic Heritage Award Foundation's Youth Awards, which went on to give $1.1 million in scholarships to more than four hundred students in twelve cities in just a six-year span. She later served as Fannie Mae's senior vice president, where she was responsible for lender relationships in twenty-eight states and for a nearly tenfold increase in business volume.

In the spring of 2004, Tallman was elected the president and general counsel of the Mexican American Legal Defense and Educational Fund (MALDEF). Upon accepting the post, she noted that her deep commit-

1979	1980	1980–88	1982
Political unrest in El Salvador, Nicaragua, and Guatemala trigger mass migrations to the United States.	The Mariel Boatlift sends 125,000 exiles to the shores of the United States in a single year after Castro announces that Cubans wishing to leave are free to do so. Cuban Americans mobilize and get a fleet of boats to pick them up.	The Number of Hispanics in the workforce increases by 48 percent, representing 20 percent of U.S. employment growth.	Colombian Gabriel García Márquez wins the Nobel Prize in Literature for *One Hundred Years of Solitude*.

ment to the community was inspired in part by experiences she had as a child standing on a picket line with her father, a factory worker who was striking with fellow workers for safer working conditions, decent wages, and health benefits.

She also spent considerable time with her mother in helping improve political access for Hispanic communities in Iowa. "These early life experiences helped define who I am, and the values I hold dear—fairness, dignity, respect for others, and justice," she said. Tallman resolved that if she was ever in a position to serve as a voice for those who did not have one, "I would be that voice."

César Estrada Chávez

No account of renowned Hispanic role models, or U.S. history, for that matter, can be complete without mention of folk hero and labor leader César Estrada Chávez, who did as much for the rights of Latino workers as did anyone throughout the twentieth century. Chavez grew up in a small adobe hut in Yuma, Arizona, and saw his father swindled in a land deal at an early age.

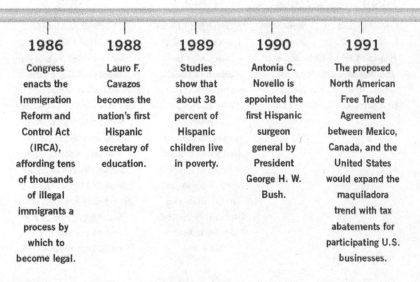

1986	1988	1989	1990	1991
Congress enacts the Immigration Reform and Control Act (IRCA), affording tens of thousands of illegal immigrants a process by which to become legal.	Lauro F. Cavazos becomes the nation's first Hispanic secretary of education.	Studies show that about 38 percent of Hispanic children live in poverty.	Antonia C. Novello is appointed the first Hispanic surgeon general by President George H. W. Bush.	The proposed North American Free Trade Agreement between Mexico, Canada, and the United States would expand the maquiladora trend with tax abatements for participating U.S. businesses.

Out of desperation, Chavez and his family moved to California, where they lived in a barrio dubbed Sal Si Puedes, or "Get Out If You Can," and worked the fields of California from Brawley to Oxnard and from Atascadero to Salinas.

Instead of attending high school, Chavez became a full-time migrant farmworker to support the family after his father was incapacitated in an accident. Nevertheless, Chavez would soon become an astute student of the human condition. In 1962, he founded the National Farm Workers Association, which later became the United Farm Workers (UFW), and made the country aware of the struggles and abuses faced by farmworkers around the land.

A true leader doesn't just issue orders, he believed. "If a leader cannot give it all, he cannot expect his people to give anything," he said. Chavez was present in every important laborer battleground. He succeeded in improving conditions through such nonviolent tactics as boycotts, pickets, and strikes. After his death in 1993, his funeral was the largest of any

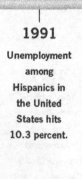

1991

Unemployment among Hispanics in the United States hits 10.3 percent.

1992

Salsa outsells ketchup as the most popular American condiment.

1993

President Bill Clinton names twenty-five Hispanics to administrative positions, including Federico Peña as secretary of transportation and Henry Cisneros as secretary of housing and urban development (HUD). Peña and Cisneros are the first Hispanics to hold the two posts.

1993

Californians pass Proposition 187, banning undocumented immigrants from receiving public education and public benefits such as subsidized health care and welfare. The measure requires teachers, doctors, and public officials to report suspected illegal aliens to the attorney general's office in California and to the Immigration and Naturalization Service (INS).

labor leader in the history of the United States Caravans from Florida to California came to pay their respects.

More Notables

While Hispanic Americans have a long history of success in soccer, baseball, golf, track and field, and other spring, summer, and fall sports, some stellar performances in traditional winter sports in recent years are opening doors for even more opportunities.

Speed skater Derek Parra became the first Mexican American to medal in the Olympic Winter Games, winning the gold with a world record performance in the 1,500-meter race and a silver medal in the 5,000-meter race in Salt Lake City. Fellow speed skater Jennifer Rodriguez was the first Cuban American to compete in any Winter Games, winning two bronze medals in the women's 1,000-meter and 1,500-meter races in Salt Lake City.

Also breaking out of old stereotypes are New Jersey Devils all-star

1994	1995	1996	1998
NAFTA takes effect.	A federal judge rules that Proposition 187 is unconstitutional. Boycotts of ABC-TV by Hispanic Americans organized in Los Angeles, Fresno, Chicago, Houston, San Francisco, and New York protest the lack of Latino-oriented programming.	California voters approve Proposition 209, banning preferential treatment based on race and gender. The initiative effectively gets rid of affirmative action in hiring, education, and public contracts in the state.	California voters approve Proposition 227, banning bilingual classroom education programs, replacing them with intensive "English immersion" programs. Displaying growing clout, African Americans and Hispanic Americans now constitute 16 percent of U.S. voters, up 4 percent from four years earlier.

center Scott Gomez, who has caught fire in the National Hockey League this decade, and ever-hustling Denver Nuggets forward Eduardo Najera of the National Basketball Association.

Among the hundreds of contemporary Latino role models that Latino children can readily look up to are musician Gloria Estefan, astronaut Ellen Ochoa, actor-comedian John Leguizamo, perennial baseball all-star Alex Rodriguez, boxer Oscar De La Hoya, and actress Jennifer Lopez. Sonia Monzano, who is better recognized as Maria Rodriguez from the classic kids show *Sesame Street*, was among the earlier role models whom young Hispanics have been able to relate to.

Presently, the influence of the Latino population is growing like no other. Latinos are projected to account for about half the growth in the U.S. labor force from 2005 to 2020 (Pew Research Center, "Trends 2005"). An estimated 8 million Latinos voted in the presidential election in 2004, and that number is only expected to grow.

Latino spending power is also on the rise, and savvy media types, marketers, and retailers are starting to pay closer attention to this growing population, whose spending power is expected to reach $1.01 billion

1999

Hispanic groups join the NAACP in protesting the lack of minority roles in prime-time shows. Studies show that more than 60 percent of Hispanics feel television doesn't accurately represent them.

1999–2000

Six-year-old Elián González is rescued off the Florida coast after his mother and ten others die trying to reach the United States from Cuba. For seven months Elián's Cuban American relatives fight to keep him in the States while his father wants him returned to Cuba. The boy finally returns to Cuba with his father in June 2000. Several Spanish-language Web sites are launched, including Spanish versions of AOL and Yahoo! Gateway invests $10 million in quepasa.com and Microsoft creates a new Spanish-language Web portal in Mexico.

in 2008. By 2008, Latinos are also expected to account for 9.6 percent of the nation's buying power, up from 5.2 percent in 1990.

Discussion Questions

1. What societal conditions or factors have contributed to the lower-than-average educational and economic standing of Latinos/Hispanics in this country?

2. How did Hispanics originate in the United States, and how does that origin differ from the arrival of other groups that are also considered immigrants?

3. How can the U.S. Hispanic population leverage its newfound status as the largest minority in the country?

4. In general, how are Hispanics portrayed in the American broadcast media? What effect does this portrayal have on Hispanic youth?

2003	2003	2006
Hispanics become the nation's largest minority group—surpassing African Americans.	Cuban-born Nilo Cruz wins the Pulitzer Prize for drama, for his play *Anna in the Tropics*.	Tens of thousands of Hispanics and immigration advocates take to the streets of America in peaceful demonstrations demanding that Congress abandon its attempts to build walls and fences along the U.S.-Mexican border and make illegal immigration a felony. The demonstrations confirm Hispanics as a political force and open new dialogue about the scope of U.S. Hispanic contributions and their impact on the U.S. economy.

Sources: Gale Free Resources, www.gale.com; Family Tree Toolkit.

SIX

African Americans

We all should know that diversity makes for a rich tapestry, and we must understand that all the threads of the tapestry are equal in value no matter what their color.

—MAYA ANGELOU

Positive changes in American race relations have lifted us all. Close to four decades after the death of Dr. Martin Luther King Jr., America has made long strides toward including people who were once labeled and treated as second-class citizens.

But in many cases, the transformation from a race-based culture into a talent-based culture can be a long process. The struggle for socioeconomic equality continues for much of the African American population. That challenge is especially evident in employment numbers, health-care statistics, and incarceration rates among today's African Americans.

More than two centuries ago, authors of the U.S. Constitution measured enslaved African Americans as 60 percent of a white person for "accounting purposes." While that practice ended long ago, today's African American—using the barometers of economics, housing, education, health, social justice, and civic engagement—measures up to just 73 percent of the average Caucasian in American society, according to the National Urban League's 2004 report, *The State of Black America: The Complexity of Black Progress.*

Looking at black America's advancement since the civil rights era, we see that fewer than half of black families own their own homes, compared to over 70 percent of whites, and that blacks are denied mortgages and home improvement loans at twice the rate of whites. Blacks are also twice as likely to die from disease, accident, and homicide at every stage of life. Life expectancy for African Americans is currently seventy-two years, versus seventy-eight years for whites.

Astonishingly, black infant mortality rates are higher today than in 1970. In 2001, that rate was fourteen deaths per one thousand live births, 146 percent higher than the white rate. Half of people age twenty-five and younger with HIV in America are black (*Washington Post,* January 23, 2004), while black unemployment rates are nearly double that for whites—10.8 percent versus 5.2 percent in the 2003 data. Additionally, a

African American Timeline

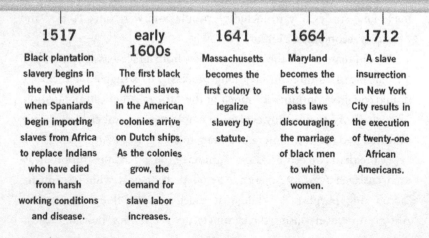

1517	early 1600s	1641	1664	1712
Black plantation slavery begins in the New World when Spaniards begin importing slaves from Africa to replace Indians who have died from harsh working conditions and disease.	The first black African slaves in the American colonies arrive on Dutch ships. As the colonies grow, the demand for slave labor increases.	Massachusetts becomes the first colony to legalize slavery by statute.	Maryland becomes the first state to pass laws discouraging the marriage of black men to white women.	A slave insurrection in New York City results in the execution of twenty-one African Americans.

black person's average jail sentence is six months longer than a white's for the same crime: thirty-nine months versus thirty-three months.

THE ECONOMICS OF DISPARITY— AND DESPAIR

Earlier in this book, we stressed that minorities in American companies need to transcend their race to succeed in our international culture and global economy. But they've got to be allowed in the door first! Only 41 percent of Fortune 1000 firms had at least one African American on their boards of directors as of 2000. Additionally, the average African American college graduate can expect to earn a half million dollars less in a lifetime than an average white college graduate. What's more, black high school graduates working full-time from age twenty-five to sixty-four will earn $300,000 less!

There are many reasons for these disparities. One is old-fashioned discrimination. Today's version is a little more veiled and subtle. A relative lack of educational options, plus a shortage of accessible and afford-

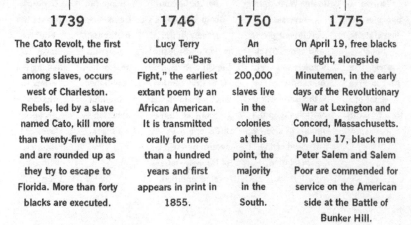

1739	1746	1750	1775
The Cato Revolt, the first serious disturbance among slaves, occurs west of Charleston. Rebels, led by a slave named Cato, kill more than twenty-five whites and are rounded up as they try to escape to Florida. More than forty blacks are executed.	Lucy Terry composes "Bars Fight," the earliest extant poem by an African American. It is transmitted orally for more than a hundred years and first appears in print in 1855.	An estimated 200,000 slaves live in the colonies at this point, the majority in the South.	On April 19, free blacks fight, alongside Minutemen, in the early days of the Revolutionary War at Lexington and Concord, Massachusetts. On June 17, black men Peter Salem and Salem Poor are commended for service on the American side at the Battle of Bunker Hill.

able health care, prevails in many of minority communities. Government actions of the past quarter century, which have funneled more money to the superrich as the bottom half struggles to stay afloat, are all part of the equation, as is an apparent racial bias in the distribution of welfare benefits.

Not to say there's no progress to note. The dropout rate for black high school students has declined 44 percent since 1968, so that now 79 percent of blacks twenty-five and older have graduated from high school, compared to just 30 percent in 1968, according to the 2004 Urban League report. Home ownership rates, while still proportionately low in this population, are rising, and income averages are up. While other ethnic groups are growing in their population and economic clout, black consumers are still outspending all other groups in apparel, food, beverages, cars and trucks, home furnishings, telephone service, and travel—wielding an increasing economic clout (Target Market News, *The Buying Power of Black America*, 2003).

In fact, by 2007, the collective spending power of America's ethnic

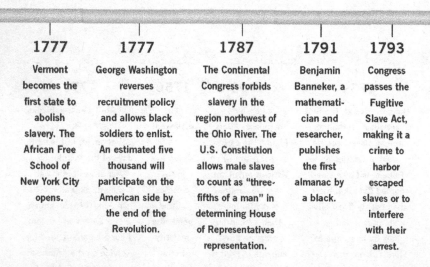

1777	1777	1787	1791	1793
Vermont becomes the first state to abolish slavery. The African Free School of New York City opens.	George Washington reverses recruitment policy and allows black soldiers to enlist. An estimated five thousand will participate on the American side by the end of the Revolution.	The Continental Congress forbids slavery in the region northwest of the Ohio River. The U.S. Constitution allows male slaves to count as "three-fifths of a man" in determining House of Representatives representation.	Benjamin Banneker, a mathematician and researcher, publishes the first almanac by a black.	Congress passes the Fugitive Slave Act, making it a crime to harbor escaped slaves or to interfere with their arrest.

minority groups will exceed $2 trillion, outpacing the growth in white consumer spending by more than 80 percent (University of Georgia's Selig Center for Economic Growth, *The Multicultural Economy: Minority Buying Power 2003*). African American buying power, which was $688 billion in 2003, is expected to hit $921 billion in 2008. By 2008, African Americans are expected to account for 8.7 percent of the country's buying power, up from 7.4 percent in 1990.

LABELS

Among the biggest overriding factors impeding economic and social progress is the myth that everyone started on an equal footing in the United States. Just scan the timeline in this chapter for confirmation. As African Americans have made headway in their struggle for personal and fiscal independence, they've had to overcome more obstacles than any other ethnic group in this country's history. Those barriers not only include generations of forced slavery and subservience, but a succession

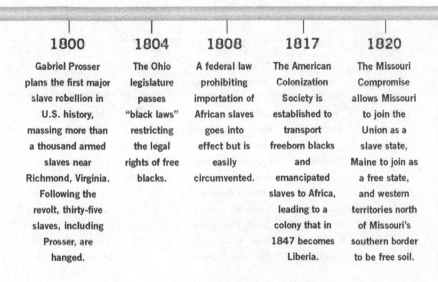

1800	1804	1808	1817	1820
Gabriel Prosser plans the first major slave rebellion in U.S. history, massing more than a thousand armed slaves near Richmond, Virginia. Following the revolt, thirty-five slaves, including Prosser, are hanged.	The Ohio legislature passes "black laws" restricting the legal rights of free blacks.	A federal law prohibiting importation of African slaves goes into effect but is easily circumvented.	The American Colonization Society is established to transport freeborn blacks and emancipated slaves to Africa, leading to a colony that in 1847 becomes Liberia.	The Missouri Compromise allows Missouri to join the Union as a slave state, Maine to join as a free state, and western territories north of Missouri's southern border to be free soil.

of stereotypes and slurs that seem to linger and survive by changing shape.

NEVER: *nigger, negress, negroid, colored, mulatto, dark continent, brown sugar, Aunt Jemima, Oreo, Uncle Tom, buck, boy*

BE CAREFUL WITH: *Negro, African, mixed-race, ghetto, nigga, Black Muslim*

BEST: *African American, black, biracial, urban, Muslim*

Nigger, of course, has carried deep-seated and painfully racist connotations since slavery. *Nigga* has gained traction in recent years in the entertainment culture. Many consider it a slur, no matter the spelling, but others don't. In fact, some African Americans are neutral on it, even to the point where it is used by some affectionately. It is best avoided, however.

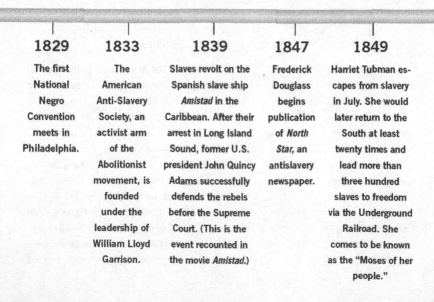

1829	1833	1839	1847	1849
The first National Negro Convention meets in Philadelphia.	The American Anti-Slavery Society, an activist arm of the Abolitionist movement, is founded under the leadership of William Lloyd Garrison.	Slaves revolt on the Spanish slave ship *Amistad* in the Caribbean. After their arrest in Long Island Sound, former U.S. president John Quincy Adams successfully defends the rebels before the Supreme Court. (This is the event recounted in the movie *Amistad*.)	Frederick Douglass begins publication of *North Star,* an antislavery newspaper.	Harriet Tubman escapes from slavery in July. She would later return to the South at least twenty times and lead more than three hundred slaves to freedom via the Underground Railroad. She comes to be known as the "Moses of her people."

Be very careful with context. *Negro,* once in common use, is now archaic and can be offensive to some, unless used in reference to organization names and in historical references such as to the National Council of Negro Women or the Negro Leagues. *Negress,* however, is generally a slur. *Colored,* also once a part of the common lexicon, is outdated and often a slur, though it is acceptable in the names of organizations such as the National Association for the Advancement of Colored People.

The terms *African American* and *black* are suggested. You should employ the term *African* only in reference to a person who is from Africa. Terms such as *mixed-race* and *mulatto* when used to describe people with white and black parents or those with parents of different ethnic ancestry are best avoided. It's better to use *biracial.* In general, the issue of a person's race, sexual orientation, or religion should not be raised in conversation or print unless it is relevant. This principle also applies to references to ethnicity.

Animal references such as *monkey* and *bunny,* when applied to people, reek of racism. *Buck,* a slave-era term for a strong and healthy black male,

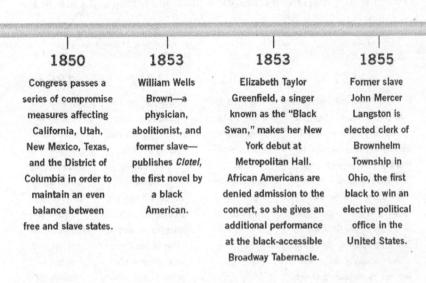

1850	1853	1853	1855
Congress passes a series of compromise measures affecting California, Utah, New Mexico, Texas, and the District of Columbia in order to maintain an even balance between free and slave states.	William Wells Brown—a physician, abolitionist, and former slave— publishes *Clotel,* the first novel by a black American.	Elizabeth Taylor Greenfield, a singer known as the "Black Swan," makes her New York debut at Metropolitan Hall. African Americans are denied admission to the concert, so she gives an additional performance at the black-accessible Broadway Tabernacle.	Former slave John Mercer Langston is elected clerk of Brownhelm Township in Ohio, the first black to win an elective political office in the United States.

is an ugly term that has faded, fortunately. "Aunt Jemima," a promotional figure based on a "pancake queen" image that was drawn from a real former slave, is considered a highly negative stereotype of black women and a slur. *Shvartzer,* a Yiddish term for blacks, is often used derogatorily.

Brown sugar has grown to be an insulting characterization for black women, while *Oreo* is a disparaging term for a black person said to be "white on the inside." It's a latter-day version of the "Uncle Tom" name. Then there are other old, mean-spirited terms labeling African Americans (*Sambo, coon, jig, pickaninny,* etc.) whose users know they are always patently offensive.

The *dark continent* as a name for Africa can also be offensive in its double meaning and is best avoided. *Ghetto,* once commonly used, has come to carry a strong negative connotation as a section of a city inhabited only by minorities. *Urban* is more acceptable. Using the specific name of the neighborhood is even better. *Black Muslim* should just be *Muslim.*

People in the media and other communicators should employ some caution when using race or ethnicity to describe a person as the first to ac-

1857	1861	1862	1862
In the *Dred Scott* decision, the Supreme Court holds that Congress cannot prohibit slavery in the territories, that black people are not citizens, and that residence in a free state doesn't confer freedom on them. The decision hastens the start of the Civil War by inciting anger in the North and sweeping aside legal barriers to expanding slavery.	The Civil War begins in Charleston, South Carolina, as Confederates open fire on Fort Sumter.	The second of two Confiscation Acts is passed, stating that slaves of civilian and military Confederate officials "shall be forever free." It is enforceable only in areas of the South that are occupied by the Union Army.	On July 17, Congress allows the enlistment of blacks in the Union Army. An estimated 186,000 blacks serve, and 38,000 of those soldiers die.

complish a feat. While firsts are important, and rarely offensive when pointed out, race and ethnicity shouldn't be overemphasized in many cases because it may make an achievement seem like it is dependent on only race, not ability. Reserve mention of race largely for significant and groundbreaking appointments and achievements, awards, and historical biographies. It fits well for Pulitzer or Nobel Prize winners, cabinet appointments, major elected offices, judgeships, or other high positions, or major sports achievements and firsts, or entertainment awards that once seemed out of reach of minorities (for example, Halle Berry's becoming the first African American woman to win the Best Actress Academy Award).

Be mindful of other language nuances. For example, calling a minority person "articulate" can imply that it is an exceptional occurrence for a person of color to speak clearly and knowledgeably on a topic. People who refer to an African American as someone "who happens to be black" may happen to be revealing their bigotry. Economist Thomas Sowell once wisecracked about people who refer to him in those terms: "I wonder if they realize that both my parents are black. If I had turned out

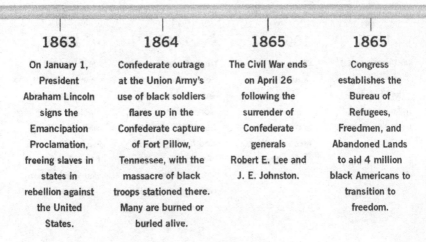

1863

On January 1, President Abraham Lincoln signs the Emancipation Proclamation, freeing slaves in states in rebellion against the United States.

1864

Confederate outrage at the Union Army's use of black soldiers flares up in the Confederate capture of Fort Pillow, Tennessee, with the massacre of black troops stationed there. Many are burned or buried alive.

1865

The Civil War ends on April 26 following the surrender of Confederate generals Robert E. Lee and J. E. Johnston.

1865

Congress establishes the Bureau of Refugees, Freedmen, and Abandoned Lands to aid 4 million black Americans to transition to freedom.

to be Scandinavian or Chinese, people would have wondered what was going on."

In some neighborhoods, law enforcement officials and others who should know better flippantly refer to African Americans as "perps," short for "perpetrators." Not long ago, photographer Harris Hartsfield cleverly addressed the labeling of African Americans as criminals in one of his exhibitions. He photographed black doctors, lawyers, and other professionals mug-shot-style and wearing plain white T-shirts, then placed their résumés in small print next to each photo. Many people entering the gallery mentally mislabeled the pictured characters as criminals from a distance and seemed shocked and wide-eyed to find the group members were actually community role models.

Some may remember the classic social experiment showing that white interviewers not only sat farther away from black job applicants than from white applicants, they kept the session 25 percent shorter and made more speech errors during the interview. The point was that anyone of any background treated in such a manner is bound to fare poorly in the job interview process.

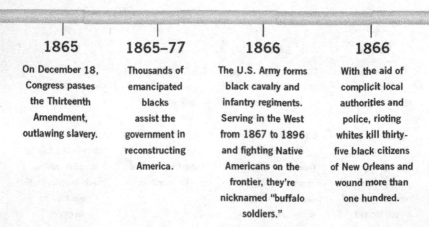

1865	1865–77	1866	1866
On December 18, Congress passes the Thirteenth Amendment, outlawing slavery.	Thousands of emancipated blacks assist the government in reconstructing America.	The U.S. Army forms black cavalry and infantry regiments. Serving in the West from 1867 to 1896 and fighting Native Americans on the frontier, they're nicknamed "buffalo soldiers."	With the aid of complicit local authorities and police, rioting whites kill thirty-five black citizens of New Orleans and wound more than one hundred.

CHALLENGES

There's still a lot of room for American institutions to transform by embracing equity for the African American population.

In 2002, African Americans nationally were incarcerated at seven times the rate of whites (Justice Policy Institute, 2003). African Americans and Latinos combined made up 68 percent of all prisoners in 2002, even though African Americans and Latinos make up only 25 percent of the U.S. population. Further, while African American men represent 6 percent of the population, they constitute 44 percent of the prison population.

In one glaring illustration, African Americans represent just 28 percent of Maryland's population, but constitute 90 percent of the people in prison for drug offenses in the state and 68 percent of those arrested for drug offenses, even though national studies show that whites and blacks use drugs at similar rates. These imprisonment rates only serve to separate fathers and mothers from their children and promote a never-ending cycle of despair.

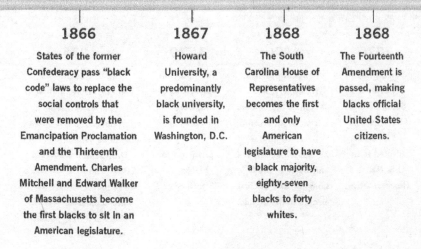

1866	1867	1868	1868
States of the former Confederacy pass "black code" laws to replace the social controls that were removed by the Emancipation Proclamation and the Thirteenth Amendment. Charles Mitchell and Edward Walker of Massachusetts become the first blacks to sit in an American legislature.	Howard University, a predominantly black university, is founded in Washington, D.C.	The South Carolina House of Representatives becomes the first and only American legislature to have a black majority, eighty-seven blacks to forty whites.	The Fourteenth Amendment is passed, making blacks official United States citizens.

In the good-news/bad-news department, the U.S. Senate apologized in June 2005 for failing to enact federal antilynching legislation decades earlier—capping a century-old effort initiated by George Henry White, the founder of my hometown of Whitesboro, New Jersey. While no legislation can truly atone for the nearly five thousand people lynched in America from the post–Civil War period through the middle of the twentieth century, the long-stalled resolution was at least an acknowledgment that the Senate should have acted long ago to rid the country of those reprehensible acts that were used to control and intimidate African Americans.

Over the generations, Congress was asked by seven presidents to enact a statute making lynching a federal crime. The U.S. House did its part on three occasions by passing legislation, but the Senate always said no, caving to filibusters by southern senators. The 2005 resolution was passed by voice vote because some southern senators apparently didn't want to go on record to apologize for past crimes. Twenty senators initially refused to support the resolution or participate in the roll-call vote. Ten of those later added their names to the action.

On that dicey subject, *Miami Herald* syndicated columnist Leonard

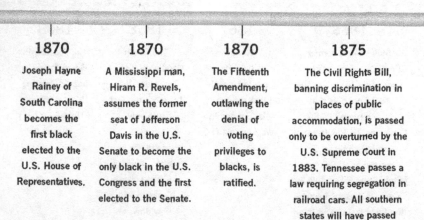

1870	1870	1870	1875
Joseph Hayne Rainey of South Carolina becomes the first black elected to the U.S. House of Representatives.	A Mississippi man, Hiram R. Revels, assumes the former seat of Jefferson Davis in the U.S. Senate to become the only black in the U.S. Congress and the first elected to the Senate.	The Fifteenth Amendment, outlawing the denial of voting privileges to blacks, is ratified.	The Civil Rights Bill, banning discrimination in places of public accommodation, is passed only to be overturned by the U.S. Supreme Court in 1883. Tennessee passes a law requiring segregation in railroad cars. All southern states will have passed similar laws by 1907.

Pitts Jr. wrote in June 2005, "The moral cowardice of 20 holdout senators aside, how much political courage is required in 2005 to say it is wrong to stand by as mobs murder people? What does it tell you that we must get almost 50 years beyond lynching before we can muster the fortitude to call the sin a sin?"

LEADERS

Harriet Tubman

There are few stories of struggle that surpass the heroic tale of Harriet Tubman, a woman who transcended the shackles of her time to become a pioneer in the cause of freedom.

Born into slavery as Harriet Ross in 1819 or 1820 in Dorchester County, Maryland, Harriet Tubman was raised under very harsh conditions and was often subject to whipping as a small child. At age twelve, Tubman was hit in the head by a white overseer for refusing to help tie up a man who had attempted escape.

The blow saddled her with a form of narcolepsy the rest of her life. At

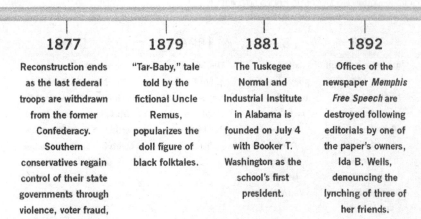

1877	1879	1881	1892
Reconstruction ends as the last federal troops are withdrawn from the former Confederacy. Southern conservatives regain control of their state governments through violence, voter fraud, and intimidation.	"Tar-Baby," tale told by the fictional Uncle Remus, popularizes the doll figure of black folktales.	The Tuskegee Normal and Industrial Institute in Alabama is founded on July 4 with Booker T. Washington as the school's first president.	Offices of the newspaper *Memphis Free Speech* are destroyed following editorials by one of the paper's owners, Ida B. Wells, denouncing the lynching of three of her friends.

age twenty-five, she married a free African American, John Tubman. Fearing she'd be sold south, Tubman escaped to freedom in Pennsylvania, where she soon became a conductor in the Underground Railroad network, eventually basing her operations in Canada and working long hours at various jobs to finance her activities.

Tubman returned to Maryland to rescue other enslaved members of her family. In close association with abolitionists Frederick Douglass and John Brown, she is believed to have shepherded at least three hundred slaves to freedom in the North through a complex network of silent allies. Tubman did so with a grim determination that historians note was "wholly devoid of personal fear" (William Still, *The Underground Railroad*, 1871). She would be absent months at a time, running daily risk of capture by slave hunters. Tubman would come to be known as "the Moses of her people."

After the outbreak of the Civil War, Tubman served as a soldier, spy, and nurse. But she was denied payment for her wartime services and was forced to ride in a baggage car on her return trip to her home in Auburn, New York. There she became an active supporter of women's rights, and in 1908, she built a structure that would serve both as her home and as a

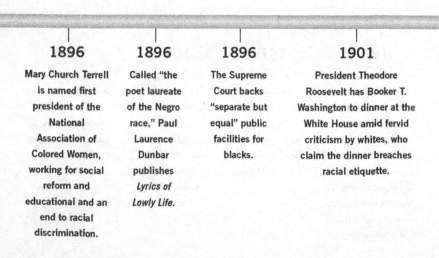

1896	1896	1896	1901
Mary Church Terrell is named first president of the National Association of Colored Women, working for social reform and educational and an end to racial discrimination.	Called "the poet laureate of the Negro race," Paul Laurence Dunbar publishes *Lyrics of Lowly Life.*	The Supreme Court backs "separate but equal" public facilities for blacks.	President Theodore Roosevelt has Booker T. Washington to dinner at the White House amid fervid criticism by whites, who claim the dinner breaches racial etiquette.

home for the aged and indigent. There she worked until her death in 1913.

Tubman was buried in Auburn with military honors. A prominent vessel, the Liberty ship *Harriet Tubman,* was christened in 1944 by Eleanor Roosevelt. In 1995, Tubman was honored by a U.S. Postal Service commemorative stamp bearing her name and likeness. Harriet Tubman was not only a leader; she literally led hundreds to freedom.

George Washington Carver

It's a rare day that a U.S. citizen doesn't benefit from inventions or research by another trailblazer, the brilliant agricultural chemist George Washington Carver. When the former slave died at age seventy-nine on January 5, 1943, his stamp was indelibly etched on everyday life around the globe.

Born into slavery in Diamond Grove, Missouri, Carver and his mother were kidnapped by Confederate raiders during the Civil War. Carver's master, Moses Carver, finally located him but not his mother, so Moses and his wife decided to raise him. Carver later left the family and went to work as a farmhand, graduating from high school in Kansas be-

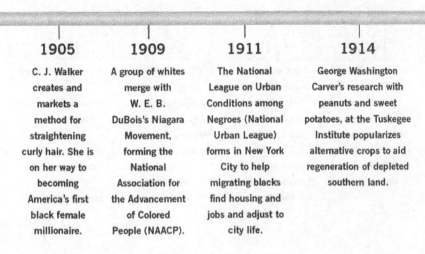

1905	1909	1911	1914
C. J. Walker creates and markets a method for straightening curly hair. She is on her way to becoming America's first black female millionaire.	A group of whites merge with W. E. B. DuBois's Niagara Movement, forming the National Association for the Advancement of Colored People (NAACP).	The National League on Urban Conditions among Negroes (National Urban League) forms in New York City to help migrating blacks find housing and jobs and adjust to city life.	George Washington Carver's research with peanuts and sweet potatoes, at the Tuskegee Institute popularizes alternative crops to aid regeneration of depleted southern land.

fore becoming the first black student to enter Simpson College. He transferred to Iowa Agricultural College (now Iowa State University), where he received his BS in agricultural science and MS in agriculture.

After graduation, Carver took a faculty position at Iowa College. But Booker T. Washington offered him a post at the new Tuskegee Normal and Industrial Institute for Negroes in 1897 and Carver accepted. While at Tuskegee, Carver developed a crop rotation method that alternated cotton with such soil-enriching plantings as peanuts, sweet potatoes, and pecans. He developed over three hundred uses for peanuts and dozens of uses for other crops and products.

Among Carver's inventions were adhesives, bleach, chili sauce, cream, dyes, flour, ink, instant coffee, insulation board, linoleum, mayonnaise, paper, shampoo, shoe polish, shaving cream, sugar, synthetic rubber, and talcum powder. Carver only patented three inventions, desiring to make his ideas and findings available to everyone. A humble leader, he bequeathed all his life savings to the George Washington Carver Foundation upon his death. His life is commemorated by a national monument and other markers, but it is his multiple contributions to humanity that ensure his lasting memory.

1917

Antagonism toward blacks employed in war-related industries spurs riots in East Saint Louis, Illinois, that kill forty blacks and eight whites.

1919

Two weeks of racial violence in Chicago kill 23 blacks and 15 whites and injure 537 while rendering 1,000 black families homeless.

1922

Bessie Coleman stages the first public flight by an African American woman. She refuses to perform in front of racially segregated audiences.

1925

An estimated fifty thousand unmasked Ku Klux Klan members march in Washington, D.C. Nationally, Klan membership exceeds 4 million.

Dr. Martin Luther King Jr.

No mention of African American leaders—past or present—could be complete without Dr. Martin Luther King Jr., a man whose legacy lives on in the hearts of millions. His tale began with his birth as a pastor's son in Atlanta, Georgia. He was ordained in 1947 and became minister of a Baptist church in Montgomery, Alabama. He led the black boycott of segregated city bus lines and gained a major victory and prestige as a civil rights leader in 1956 when Montgomery buses desegregated. He said, "The arc of the moral universe is long but it bends toward justice as long as we help bend it that way."

King's Southern Christian Leadership Conference gave him a home base to pursue further nonviolent civil rights resistance activities nationwide. His philosophy led to his arrest on numerous occasions in the 1950s and '60s. King led a peaceful 1963 protest in Birmingham that brought him worldwide attention. And of course, he headed the historic March on Washington in August 1963.

King was awarded the Nobel Peace Prize in 1964. On April 4, 1968, he was shot and killed as he stood on the balcony of the Lorraine Motel in

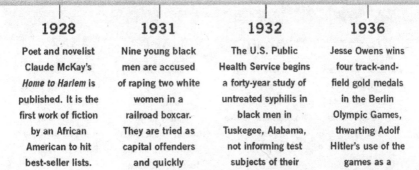

1928	1931	1932	1936
Poet and novelist Claude McKay's *Home to Harlem* is published. It is the first work of fiction by an African American to hit best-seller lists.	Nine young black men are accused of raping two white women in a railroad boxcar. They are tried as capital offenders and quickly convicted.	The U.S. Public Health Service begins a forty-year study of untreated syphilis in black men in Tuskegee, Alabama, not informing test subjects of their disease or participation in the inhumane test.	Jesse Owens wins four track-and-field gold medals in the Berlin Olympic Games, thwarting Adolf Hitler's use of the games as a display of Aryan supremacy.

Memphis. His birthday is a national holiday, celebrated on the third Monday in January.

His electrifying oratory resounds as if delivered yesterday. In his 1961 message to the AFL-CIO, a forerunner to his classic "I Have a Dream" speech in Washington a few years later, King said he looked forward with confidence to a day when all workers would labor side by side with "no thought to their separateness as Negroes, Jews, Italians or any other distinctions." On that day, he said, all citizens will fully realize the American dream of equal opportunity, equal privilege, and equal property rights, and dignify all humans without the argument "that the color of a man's skin determines the content of his character."

That day, it seems, is arriving.

Oprah Winfrey

Someone whom I know about firsthand, who has with her leadership created the standard for many of us to follow, and who was born in Kosciusko, Mississippi, Oprah Winfrey suffered abuse and molestation in the home of her mother. When she ran away from home at age thirteen, she was looking at a bleak future. Sent to a juvenile detention facility, she was denied admission because all the beds were full. As a last resort, she

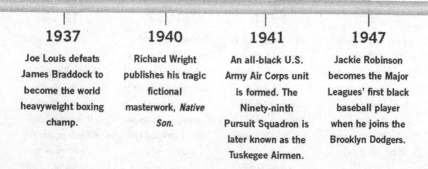

1937

Joe Louis defeats James Braddock to become the world heavyweight boxing champ.

1940

Richard Wright publishes his tragic fictional masterwork, *Native Son*.

1941

An all-black U.S. Army Air Corps unit is formed. The Ninety-ninth Pursuit Squadron is later known as the Tuskegee Airmen.

1947

Jackie Robinson becomes the Major Leagues' first black baseball player when he joins the Brooklyn Dodgers.

was sent to Nashville to live with her disciplinarian father, who imposed early curfews and other strict rules. One rule was that she read at least one book a week and sit down to write a report on it. From there, she learned rapidly. Local radio station WVOL in Nashville took a chance on the teen, who had graduated a year early from high school, and hired her at the age of seventeen. Two years later, while attending Tennessee State University as a speech, communications, and performing arts major, Winfrey signed on with WTVF-TV in Nashville, where she became the first African American woman—and the youngest person—to anchor the news there.

To say that this young woman made the most of her turnabout is at best an understatement. Through the power of the airwaves and her positive message, Winfrey has gone on to enlighten, entertain, and inspire millions for three decades and become one of the most influential celebrities in the world. Her accomplishments as an actor, television pioneer, producer, publisher, educator, and philanthropist make her a leading role model for both African Americans and a diverse audience worldwide. Her top-rated *Oprah Winfrey Show* is seen by an estimated 30 million viewers a week in the United States and is broadcast internationally in 111 countries. Winfrey's acting debut in the 1985 Steven Spielberg

1948	1950	1954	1955
Legendary Negro Leagues Star Satchel Paige is finally allowed a chance to pitch in the Major Leagues.	Gwendolyn Brooks becomes the first African American to win the Pulitzer Prize for poetry.	The U.S. Supreme Court rules unanimously in *Brown v. Board of Education of Topeka* that racial segregation in public schools violates the Fourteenth Amendment to the Constitution.	Lynchings continue in the South with the brutal slaying of a fourteen-year-old Chicago youth in Money, Mississippi. *Jet* magazine publishes a picture of the mutilated corpse.

film *The Color Purple* netted her Academy Award and Golden Globe nominations.

Winfrey became the first African American woman to become a billionaire; she was named to *Forbes* magazine's annual list of billionaires in 2003, only the second African American to make the prestigious list. (The first was Black Entertainment Television founder Robert Johnson.)

Over the years Winfrey has branched out into publishing (*O, The Oprah Magazine,* and the 600,000-member-strong Oprah's Book Club), producing (through Harpo Films, part of her multifaceted Harpo Entertainment Group), programming creation (for Dr. Phil and others), cable TV (Oxygen Media women's interactive channel), philanthropy, and many other endeavors.

Like George Henry White, the founder of my hometown, Winfrey has long believed that education opens the door to freedom and a brighter future. She has awarded hundreds of grants to organizations in support of education and empowerment for women, children, and families in the United States and abroad through her private charity, the Oprah Winfrey Foundation. She has donated millions to improve educa-

1955	1955	1957	1957
Rosa Parks, secretary of the Montgomery, Alabama, chapter of the NAACP, refuses to surrender her seat when ordered by a local bus driver, leading to the Montgomery bus boycott of 1955–56.	Singer, songwriter, and guitarist Chuck Berry records "Maybellene," a hit that helps shape the evolution of rock and roll	The Southern Christian Leadership Conference is established by the Reverend Martin Luther King Jr. and others to coordinate organizations working for full equality of African Americans.	President Dwight D. Eisenhower orders federal troops to Little Rock, Arkansas, after unsuccessfully trying to persuade Governor Orval Faubus to give up efforts to block desegregation at Central High.

tion for students who have the merit but not the means, and she has developed schools that educate thousands of underserved children internationally. Winfrey also created the Oprah Winfrey Scholars Program, which awards scholarships to students who are determined to use their education to give back to their communities in America and around the world.

Her Oprah's Angel Network, created in 1998 following an episode of *The Oprah Winfrey Show* where she encouraged viewers to make a difference in the lives of others, has raised more than $30 million to establish scholarships, schools, youth centers, homes, and women's shelters. Winfrey expanded her foundation's global humanitarian efforts with the ChristmasKindness South Africa 2002 initiative, which provided 50,000 South African children in orphanages and rural schools with gifts of food, clothes, shoes, school supplies, books, and toys, while creating sixty-three new school libraries and teacher-training programs. Her new Oprah Winfrey Leadership Academy for Girls—South Africa was built in partnership with South Africa's Ministry of Education.

Among numerous other distinctions, Winfrey's talk show has won

1957	1959	1960	1963
Congress passes the Voting Rights Bill of 1957, the first major civil rights legislation in more than seventy-five years.	Singer-songwriter Ray Charles records "What'd I say," exemplifying the emergence of soul music, combining rhythm and blues with gospel.	The sit-in movement is launched in Greensboro, North Carolina, when black college students insist on service at a local segregated lunch counter.	Medgar Evers, Mississippi field secretary for the NAACP, is shot and killed in an ambush at his home, following a historic broadcast on the subject of civil rights by President John F. Kennedy.

dozens of Emmys, she is routinely named to *Time* magazine's "100 Most Influential People in the World" list, and she was enshrined in the NAACP's Hall of Fame in 2005. Humanitarian honors include the 2004 Global Humanitarian Action Award from the United Nations Association of the United States of America.

Winfrey could have easily succumbed to her early-life challenges and difficult circumstances. Instead, she saw possibilities for herself and for countless others. She strived to create a "life brand" that has since elevated thousands around the world to the road of self-discovery. One of my favorite Oprah Winfrey quotes: "It doesn't matter who you are or where you come from. The ability to triumph begins with you. Always."

Maya Angelou

Other modern-day role models include the wondrous Maya Angelou, born Marguerite Johnson in a segregated area of Saint Louis, Missouri, in 1928. Her parents soon divorced, and her young life got much worse from there. On a visit to her mother's home at age eight, she was raped by

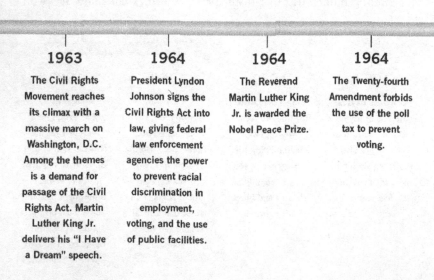

1963	1964	1964	1964
The Civil Rights Movement reaches its climax with a massive march on Washington, D.C. Among the themes is a demand for passage of the Civil Rights Act. Martin Luther King Jr. delivers his "I Have a Dream" speech.	President Lyndon Johnson signs the Civil Rights Act into law, giving federal law enforcement agencies the power to prevent racial discrimination in employment, voting, and the use of public facilities.	The Reverend Martin Luther King Jr. is awarded the Nobel Peace Prize.	The Twenty-fourth Amendment forbids the use of the poll tax to prevent voting.

her mother's boyfriend. Though she kept silent about the incident, an uncle on her mother's side found out and killed the man. Angelou went into a shell and barely spoke for four years, believing her words killed her attacker. Still in recovery, she became an unwed mother at sixteen. But Angelou soon learned to cope with those painful life events through the self-expression of her poetry. She found her voice again.

But to make ends meet in the meantime, she served as a waitress, cook, and nightclub singer for years, before progressing to dancer and actor. Along the way, she served as San Francisco's first African American streetcar conductor. In 1971, she became the first black woman to get an original screenplay, *Georgia, Georgia,* produced. She also starred in several plays.

Along the way, Angelou learned five languages and fought for civil rights alongside Martin Luther King Jr. Later, while living abroad in Cairo, she became the associate editor of *the Arab Observer,* the only English-language newsweekly in the Middle East. And of course, her poetry was heralded worldwide. She received Pulitzer Prize nominations

1964	**1965**	**1965**	**1965**
Malcolm X announces his split from Elijah Muhammad's Nation of Islam.	The Voting Rights Act is passed after the Selma-to-Montgomery March draws the nation's attention when marchers are savagely beaten by Alabama state troopers.	Malcolm X is assassinated in Harlem by Nation of Islam members.	In August, the Watts neighborhood of Los Angeles explodes into violence after a young male motorist is charged with reckless driving. In ten days of riots, thirty-four are killed, 1,032 injured, and nearly 4,000 arrested.

for her poetic works *Just Give Me a Cool Drink of Water 'fore I Diiie* (1971) and *And Still I Rise* (1976). Her autobiographical books, including *I Know Why the Caged Bird Sings, Gather Together in My Name, Singin' and Swingin' and Gettin' Merry Like Christmas,* and *The Heart of a Woman,* have won a wallful of awards.

Angelou has been a favorite of U.S. presidents. She was appointed by President Gerald Ford to the Bicentennial Commission and by President Jimmy Carter to the National Commission on the Observance of International Women's Year. Upon the request of Bill Clinton, she wrote the poem "On the Pulse of the Morning" for his 1993 presidential inauguration. Clinton's "favorite living poet" read the poem at the celebration. Today she continues to lead. Her ongoing personal outreach to improve Third World conditions has helped thousands of underprivileged women change their lives.

Leonard Pitts Jr.

Mr. Pitts, known for his fresh and passionate insights that speak to ordinary people on divisive issues, won the 2004 Pulitzer Prize for Commentary and stands out as an exemplary role model in the African American community. His rise since hiring on as pop music critic at the *Miami*

1966

The Black Panther Party for Self-Defense is founded in Oakland, California, by Bobby Seale and Huey Newton to protect blacks from police brutality.

1966

Civil rights activist Stokely Carmichael of the Southern Christian Leadership Conference introduces the phrase "black power" at a rally in Mississippi.

1966

NBA great Bill Russell becomes the first black coach of a major U.S. pro sports team (when he takes over the reins for the Boston Celtics.

1966

The African American holiday of Kwanzaa is created by Maulana Karenga, a professor at California State University at Long Beach.

Herald in 1991 has been meteoric. Pitts was first nominated for a Pulitzer in 1992. By 1994, he was writing about race and current affairs in his own column, which would become nationally syndicated. In 1999, his book *Becoming Dad: Black Men and the Journey to Fatherhood* became a best seller.

Pitts, known for not pulling any punches, was the second black journalist in as many years to win the Pulitzer for Commentary, after Colbert King of the *Washington Post* in 2003. Previously, African American writers E. R. Shipp of the New York *Daily News* (1996), William Raspberry of the *Washington Post* (1994), and Clarence Page of the *Chicago Tribune* (1989) all won in that category.

Pitts has also racked up awards from the Society of Professional Journalists, the National Association of Black Journalists, the American Association of Sunday and Feature Editors, and the Simon Wiesenthal Center and many others. He taught journalism at Hampton University as the Scripps Howard Visiting Professional award winner in 2004—the same year he won the Pulitzer.

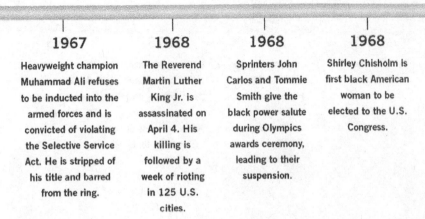

1967	1968	1968	1968
Heavyweight champion Muhammad Ali refuses to be inducted into the armed forces and is convicted of violating the Selective Service Act. He is stripped of his title and barred from the ring.	The Reverend Martin Luther King Jr. is assassinated on April 4. His killing is followed by a week of rioting in 125 U.S. cities.	Sprinters John Carlos and Tommie Smith give the black power salute during Olympics awards ceremony, leading to their suspension.	Shirley Chisholm is first black American woman to be elected to the U.S. Congress.

Barack Obama

Today new social and political leaders are emerging. One is Illinois's Barack Obama, whose 2004 landslide victory in the U.S. senatorial race gave him the sole seat held by an African American in the Senate, the fifth such seat in U.S. history and the third since Reconstruction. Obama won the election with 70 percent of the vote.

Obama studied law at Harvard University, where he was elected the first black president of the *Harvard Law Review.* He graduated magna cum laude and became a senior lecturer in constitutional law at the University of Chicago Law School.

During his tenure as a state legislator, Obama helped author a state earned income tax credit program providing benefits to the working poor, and he worked hard for legislation that would cover residents who could not afford health insurance. He successfully helped pass bills to increase funding for AIDS prevention and care programs. As keynote speaker of the 2004 Democratic National Convention, he delivered a hallmark "audacity of hope" speech that will be talked about for years.

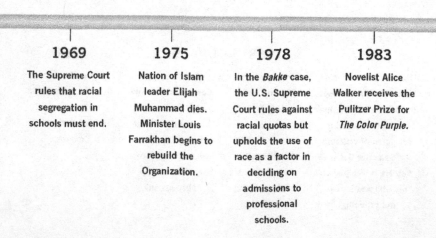

1969	1975	1978	1983
The Supreme Court rules that racial segregation in schools must end.	Nation of Islam leader Elijah Muhammad dies. Minister Louis Farrakhan begins to rebuild the Organization.	In the *Bakke* case, the U.S. Supreme Court rules against racial quotas but upholds the use of race as a factor in deciding on admissions to professional schools.	Novelist Alice Walker receives the Pulitzer Prize for *The Color Purple.*

Shaquille O'Neal

Basketball superstar Shaquille O'Neal, at seven one, still sees room for growth beyond his legendary career, which includes multiple MVP and World Champion honors and a hangar full of other roundball awards. After leaving Louisiana State University in 1992 as a junior to become a pro, he promised his mom he'd return for his degree someday. He did, in 2000.

But that wasn't enough for Shaq, who always said that sports has been a fairy-tale life for him. O'Neal earned his masters in business administration at the University of Phoenix in 2005, his size twenty-two feet tromping down the aisle alongside those of 2,200 other diploma-grabbing grads. "Someday," he said, "I'll have to put down the basketball and work a regular job. This, right here, is life. This . . . means more." Big shoes to fill!

Congratulations to Shaq and the Miami Heat on Winning the 2006 NBA Championship title.

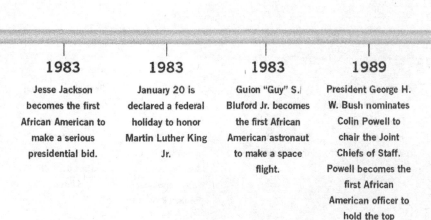

1983	1983	1983	1989
Jesse Jackson becomes the first African American to make a serious presidential bid.	January 20 is declared a federal holiday to honor Martin Luther King Jr.	Guion "Guy" S. Bluford Jr. becomes the first African American astronaut to make a space flight.	President George H. W. Bush nominates Colin Powell to chair the Joint Chiefs of Staff. Powell becomes the first African American officer to hold the top military post.

Even today, not all doors are open to people of color. Those that aren't are probably not worth entering, at least in their present state of evolutionary disrepair. You can rise above them by knowing who you are, even if those behind them do not.

Discussion Questions

1. What were some of the motivations behind earlier labels for African Americans in this country?

2. How do labels for African Americans differ now?

3. Why are some labels offensive now that weren't offensive in the past?

4. What African American leaders transcended race labels to be accepted as leaders by diverse groups of people?

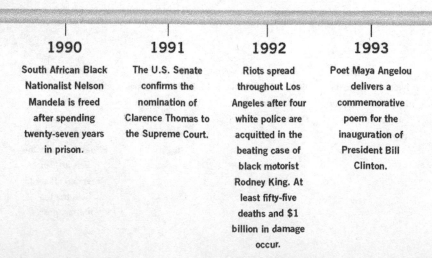

1990	1991	1992	1993
South African Black Nationalist Nelson Mandela is freed after spending twenty-seven years in prison.	The U.S. Senate confirms the nomination of Clarence Thomas to the Supreme Court.	Riots spread throughout Los Angeles after four white police are acquitted in the beating case of black motorist Rodney King. At least fifty-five deaths and $1 billion in damage occur.	Poet Maya Angelou delivers a commemorative poem for the inauguration of President Bill Clinton.

1993	1995	1997	1999
Toni Morrison wins the Nobel Prize in Literature.	Nation of Islam leader Louis Farrakhan organizes the Million Man March in Washington, D.C.	The Million Woman March draws 1.5 million black women to Philadelphia.	The NAACP calls for a boycott of South Carolina vacation destinations in an attempt to force the state to remove the Confederate flag from its statehouse.

2000

Condoleezza Rice is named foreign policy adviser for President-elect George W. Bush.

2003

The U.S. Supreme Court upholds the consideration of race in college admissions.

2004

Illinois's Barack Obama becomes the third African American to be elected to the U.S. Senate since Reconstruction.

2004

Outfielder Barry Bonds hits seven hundredth home run and goes on to break Babe Ruth's mark of 714 home runs in 2006.

2005

The U.S. Senate passes federal antilynching legislation and apologizes for blocking the law for decades. Twenty senators initially refuse to support the resolution or participate in the roll-call vote. Ten later add their names to the legislation. Nearly five thousand people—mostly African American men— were lynched between 1882 and 1968.

Sources: Gale Free Resources, www.gale.com; www.britannica.co; African-American Women's Timeline, Women's Resource Center, University of Alabama, wrc.ua.edu.

SEVEN

Asian Americans and Pacific Islanders

One day our descendants will think it incredible that we paid so much attention to things like the amount of melanin in our skin or the shape of our eyes or our gender instead of the unique identities of each of us as complex human beings.

—FRANKLIN THOMAS

"All Asians are good at . . ." "Asians are a model minority." How often do you hear such phrases in reference to modern-day Asian Americans?

Even the seemingly positive labels that characterize all Asian Americans as proficient in math and science or well-behaved as citizens are generalizations that serve to ignore the talents of many in this population. Such stereotypes have the effect of squeezing a widely diverse group into a one-size-fits-all mold.

While a far cry from some of the characterizations that other ethnic groups experience, these labels are nonetheless confining. The "model" stereotype, while superficially complimentary, glosses over problems

Asian Americans face from discrimination, creates unrealistic expectations for many, and seems to celebrate a status quo in race relations.

There's no shortage of negative stereotypes in the media in those too-rare instances when Asian Americans are seen in it. The few Asians who are depicted in television and movies are often owners of a corner grocery, a dry cleaner's, or a Chinese restaurant; are shown eating rice; have an absurdly exaggerated accent; are thrown in to provide comic relief; or are bad drivers, chronic photo snappers, karaoke jockeys, or not genuine Asians at all.

There are even more extreme caricatures such as mystical, superhuman martial artists. (You may remember the sinister Asian stereotype Dr. Fu Manchu, who had razor-sharp fingernails, flowing robes, and a cruel and ruthless mind.) Today you can see Asians in the roles of callous gang-bangers who are cool assassins on motor scooters. One popular line of motorcycles is even called Ninja.

There is some validity to the garbage-in, garbage-out theory. Psychologists have theorized that biases and distortions projected by mass media help explain why some children adopt hidden prejudices, even if their family environments strictly oppose them. All of the stereotypical depictions make it more difficult for other U.S. population groups to transform their view of Asian Americans to one of equals and for Asian Americans to not feel that they are considered foreigners in their own place of birth.

A study commissioned by Children Now shows that just 16 percent of Asian children see their race "very often" on television, compared to 70 percent of whites, 42 percent of African Americans and 22 percent of Latinos. One survey ("American Attitudes toward Chinese Americans and Asian Americans," 2001) reports that a fourth of Americans entertained "very negative" attitudes and stereotypes concerning Asian Americans.

LABELS

There's certainly no shortage of ethnic slurs for Asian Americans, such as conspicuously derogatory names like *gook* for Vietnamese, *chink* for Chinese, *Jap* and *Nip* for Japanese, and the generic *slant, yellow, rice eater,* or *rice picker* that some people mindlessly attach to all Asians. (Astonishingly, the central Illinois town of Pekin used the name Chinks for their high school teams until 1981. The name was finally changed to Dragons after the ongoing slur became a national embarrassment.)

> NEVER: *gook, chink, Jap, Nip, yellow, chigger, FOB, charlie, dink, banana, Chinaman, Chinee, Gundhi, Buddha-head*

> BE CAREFUL WITH: *Oriental*

> BEST: *Asian American, Asian (in general reference) or specific ethnicity: Japanese American, Chinese American, etc.*

Some once-accepted terms, such as *Chinaman,* now skew to the pejorative side, as do the more contemporary words *chigger* or *chigga,* slang for a Chinese person who acts like an African American. The word *Oriental* is archaic and fading out of use, although some Asian-owned or Asian-themed businesses still use it. *Chinee,* an archaic singular for the plural *Chinese,* is considered offensive.

FOB ("fresh off the boat") is a derogatory term for new Asian immigrants, as well as new immigrants from other groups. *Charlie,* slang for the American enemy in the Vietnam War, the Vietcong, is also unacceptable, as is *Dink. Gundhi* (from *Gandhi*), is a derogatory term for an Indian or other South Asian. *Buddha-head* and *banana* (yellow on the outside, white on the inside) are also ethnic slurs.

The use of words like *gook* in an attempt to lump several unique Asian cultures into a single category is still surprisingly common. Senator

John McCain's use of the word to describe his treatment as a long-term prisoner of war in Vietnam shocked the Asian American community.

As a rule, the preferred generic term for Americans of Asian descent is *Asian American*. *Asian* is acceptable as a generic reference to ancestry. But being specific when referring to particular Asian American groups, i.e., Filipino Americans, Japanese Americans, Indian Americans, when possible, is more appropriate and accurate.

Actress Ming-Na of *ER* and *The Joy Luck Club* fame, a native of Macau who moved to America at age five, once said she fought feelings of isolation and inadequacy growing up in America, where she was often lumped with other Asian Americans, who were all made to feel like foreigners. That, she said, made her and others before her feel as if they didn't have a stake in contributing to building the country. "Asking for equality is not troublemaking," she has said. "It's what we deserve."

Asian American writer Merle Woo notes that most of the time when "universal" is used to describe the American culture, "it's just a euphemism for 'white,' white themes, white significance, white culture."

Asian and Pacific Islander American Timeline

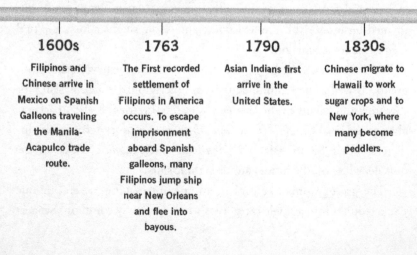

1600s	1763	1790	1830s
Filipinos and Chinese arrive in Mexico on Spanish Galleons traveling the Manila-Acapulco trade route.	The First recorded settlement of Filipinos in America occurs. To escape imprisonment aboard Spanish galleons, many Filipinos jump ship near New Orleans and flee into bayous.	Asian Indians first arrive in the United States.	Chinese migrate to Hawaii to work sugar crops and to New York, where many become peddlers.

George Takei, known as Mr. Sulu from the original *Star Trek* television series, once said that Asian Americans are viewed not so much as citizens but as "extraordinarily Americanized foreigners."

Japanese Internment

Takei learned about the importance of community from behind the barbed-wire fence of Japanese internment camps in California and Arkansas. In fact, Takei spent four years of his childhood with his family living in the two camps through this dark chapter of American history.

The Takei family's nightmare was shared by tens of thousands of fellow Japanese Americans. On February 19, 1942, just over two months after the Pearl Harbor attacks, Franklin D. Roosevelt signed Executive Order 9066, which called for the roundup of nearly 120,000 Americans of Japanese descent on the West Coast for placement in ten different internment camps—called "relocation" camps—located in Arizona, Arkansas, California, Colorado, Idaho, Utah, and Wyoming.

In addition to the post–Pearl Harbor frenzy, Roosevelt's order was fueled by anti-Japanese sentiment among farmers and other businesspeople competing against Japanese labor. In a matter of hours, tens of thousands of Japanese lost their property, possessions, pets, and savings,

1848–50	1852	1854
Gold is discovered in California. Chinese miners arrive around 1848, usually working as indentured servants. Many more Chinese immigrants arrive later to serve as cheap sources of labor for mines, railroads, and other industries. California's Foreign Miner's Tax is passed, and its enforcement is used mainly against Chinese miners, who sometimes are forced to pay the tax repeatedly.	More than 20,000 Chinese arrive in California.	The Supreme Court of California in *People v. Hall* rules that Chinese can't testify in court against whites, depriving the Chinese population of legal protections and subjecting it to acts of violence.

much of which was never to be recovered. About half of those interned were children.

Very little, if anything, about this sad episode in American history appeared in history textbooks for decades after the internment camps were finally closed in 1945. What's more, not a single case of sabotage, spying, or any other anti-American act was ever proven against any Japanese American during the entirety of World War II. Of the fewer than one dozen people who were convicted of spying for Japan in the United States, all were white! Though America was also at war with Germany and Italy, very, very few German Americans and Italian Americans were placed in the camps.

In 1988, the United States formally apologized for these internments, paying reparations to survivors while publicly stating that the incarcerations were based on "race prejudice, war hysteria, and a failure of political leadership." Limited compensation for property loss had also been paid in 1948, but at the time most former internees were unable to fully restore their losses and lives. Most were elderly or deceased by the time 1988 rolled around.

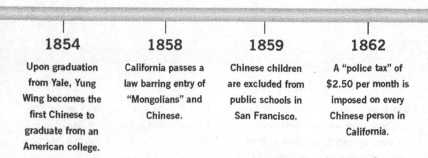

1854	1858	1859	1862
Upon graduation from Yale, Yung Wing becomes the first Chinese to graduate from an American college.	California passes a law barring entry of "Mongolians" and Chinese.	Chinese children are excluded from public schools in San Francisco.	A "police tax" of $2.50 per month is imposed on every Chinese person in California.

Two signs now posted at former U.S. Japanese internment centers summarize the government's rash actions: "Victims of war-time hysteria, these people, two-thirds of whom were United States citizens, lived a bleak humiliating life in tar paper barracks behind barbed wire and under armed guard," reads one, at Idaho's Minidoka Relocation Center 2. At another, the Poston Relocation Center 1 on the Colorado River Indian Reservation in southwestern Arizona, a sign notes, "May it serve as a constant reminder of our past so that Americans in the future will never again be denied their constitutional rights and may the remembrance of that experience serve to advance the evolution of the human spirit."

Undeterred by the camps, Takei said he drew inspiration from his stoic father and later grew to be a student of the arts, getting his big break when *Star Trek* creator Gene Roddenberry conceived the Starship *Enterprise* "as a metaphor for starship Earth." Takei later became a high-profile advocate of gay rights.

1872	1875	1880
A law in California barring Chinese court testimony is dropped.	The revised California constitution prevents corporations and municipalities from employing Chinese. The California legislature creates a law to remove Chinese outside cities' limits. The federal circuit court declares the law unconstitutional.	The United States and China sign a treaty giving the United States the right to limit Chinese immigration. The California Civil Code prohibits issuance of licenses for marriage between whites and "Mongolians, Negroes, mulattoes and persons of mixed blood."

"Foreign" Label Logic

As a rule, role models in any ethnic population are people who have actualized the values held dear by their ethnic or peer group. They've achieved what their native countrymen and countrywomen had hoped for in coming to America, while advancing some of the unifying principles that symbolize their own community's ethnicity and particular characteristics. But that desire to exert public force on the culture is largely absent in the Asian culture in the United States, many Asian Americans say.

The fact that the perpetual "foreign" label is often applied to Asians in this society has probably made the population somewhat reluctant to challenge the American structure. And failing to mount a challenge takes away the need to rise up and be heard. Some feel that a part of that quietness—that reluctance to make waves—is still a holdover from the Japanese American internment camps.

While neatly settled in as Asians in America, many Asians say they

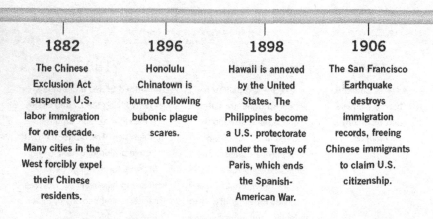

1882

The Chinese Exclusion Act suspends U.S. labor immigration for one decade. Many cities in the West forcibly expel their Chinese residents.

1896

Honolulu Chinatown is burned following bubonic plague scares.

1898

Hawaii is annexed by the United States. The Philippines become a U.S. protectorate under the Treaty of Paris, which ends the Spanish-American War.

1906

The San Francisco Earthquake destroys immigration records, freeing Chinese immigrants to claim U.S. citizenship.

don't feel fully defined as true Asian Americans. A report in the late 1990s, *An Invisible Crisis: The Educational Needs of Asian Pacific American Youth,* found that schools weren't helping the situation, offering little Asian American history in their "mainstream" programs. Vestiges of fear and discrimination remain.

LEADERS

Despite many overt instances of discrimination and marginalization, the Asian American population has stepped forward to make a firm and lasting imprint on this country's culture.

Daniel Inouye

Daniel K. Inouye, a recipient of the Congressional Medal of Honor, was the first American of Japanese descent to serve in the United States House of Representatives and Senate. As a second lieutenant, he led successful attacks on key artillery posts in Italy under heavy fire during World War

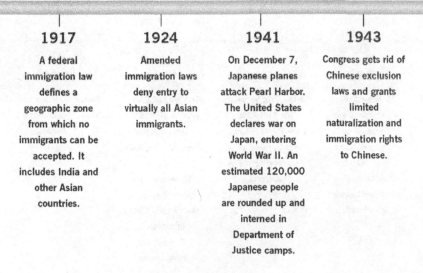

1917	1924	1941	1943
A federal immigration law defines a geographic zone from which no immigrants can be accepted. It includes India and other Asian countries.	Amended immigration laws deny entry to virtually all Asian immigrants.	On December 7, Japanese planes attack Pearl Harbor. The United States declares war on Japan, entering World War II. An estimated 120,000 Japanese people are rounded up and interned in Department of Justice camps.	Congress gets rid of Chinese exclusion laws and grants limited naturalization and immigration rights to Chinese.

II. His right arm was shattered by a grenade in the operations and later had to be amputated.

After spending twenty months in a military hospital, Inouye continued to serve the U.S. Army as a captain until he was honorably discharged in 1947, whereupon he earned his college degree and later a law degree from George Washington University. Today he is serving his seventh Senate term and is that body's third most senior member.

Besides serving as a role model for the Asian-American community, Inouye has tirelessly backed landmark legislation protecting the civil rights of people with disabilities. He was one of the original cosponsors of the Americans with Disabilities Act (ADA) of 1990, which prohibits discrimination against persons with physical or mental disability in the areas of transportation, employment, public accommodations, public services, and telecommunications.

The senator's work as honorary chairman of Hawaii's Winners at Work helped the organization establish the first community-based employment program in the state for persons with severe developmental disabilities. His actions back up his stated belief that when all people are treated with respect and dignity, everyone wins.

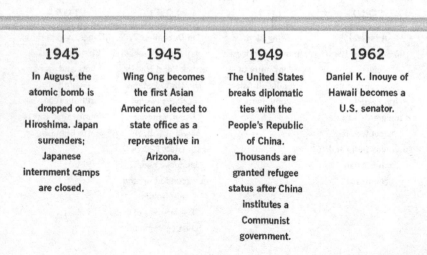

1945

In August, the atomic bomb is dropped on Hiroshima. Japan surrenders; Japanese internment camps are closed.

1945

Wing Ong becomes the first Asian American elected to state office as a representative in Arizona.

1949

The United States breaks diplomatic ties with the People's Republic of China. Thousands are granted refugee status after China institutes a Communist government.

1962

Daniel K. Inouye of Hawaii becomes a U.S. senator.

Andrea Jung

Businesswoman Andrea Jung stands out as another extraordinary role model. The oldest child of Chinese immigrants, Jung, a magna cum laude graduate of Princeton, is one of the most successful retail executives in the country. As chairman of the board and chief executive officer of Avon Products, Inc., Jung redefined the vision of the beauty products giant, leading the company into new lines of business, launching image-enhancing initiatives, and expanding opportunities for women all over the globe.

Her message of self-sufficiency is resounding: "Some people just wait for someone to take them under their wings but they should just find someone's wings to grab on to."

Originally a consultant for Avon, Jung took over as CEO there in 1999, bumping up revenues from $5.3 billion that year to $7.7 billion in 2004. She was the first woman elected to chair the Cosmetic, Toiletry, and Fragrance Association and was inducted into the Advertising Hall of Fame in 1998. *Time* magazine/CNN named her one of the "25 Most Influential Global Executives," *Business Week* named her one of the best

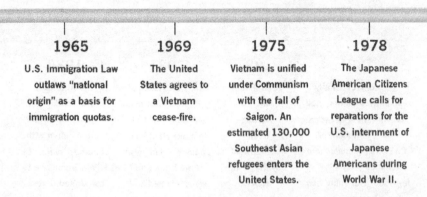

1965	1969	1975	1978
U.S. Immigration Law outlaws "national origin" as a basis for immigration quotas.	The United States agrees to a Vietnam cease-fire.	Vietnam is unified under Communism with the fall of Saigon. An estimated 130,000 Southeast Asian refugees enters the United States.	The Japanese American Citizens League calls for reparations for the U.S. internment of Japanese Americans during World War II.

managers of 2003, and she has been ranked at number three among *Fortune* magazine's "50 most powerful women in business" for two consecutive years.

In 2004, Jung was named by the *Wall Street Journal* as one of the "50 people to watch in business" and was named one of "10 prominent people to watch in 2005" by *Newsweek* magazine.

Indra Nooyi

Indra Nooyi, president and chief financial officer of PepsiCo, is another high-profile business leader. She spent her first twenty-three years growing up in India, earning her MBA from Calcutta's Indian Institute of Management before coming to the United States to attend the Yale School of Management. While attending Yale, she worked from midnight to 5 a.m. as a receptionist to make ends meet. She went to summer jobs wearing a traditional sari because she hadn't the money to buy Western clothes.

After graduation, Nooyi worked her way into several executive posts before joining PepsiCo in 1994. She was a key figure in the company's merger with Quaker Oats and was instrumental in starting PepsiCo's fast-food chains in 1997. In a talk at Dartmouth, she said that the

1981	1987	1987	1988
The congressionally established Commission on Wartime Relocation and Internment of Civilians concludes that internment was a "grave injustice" stemming from "racial prejudice, war hysteria and a failure of political leadership."	Asian Pacific American Heritage Week is established by the White House.	The U.S. House of Representatives votes 243 to 141 to make an official apology to Japanese Americans who were interned and to pay surviving internees $20,000 each in reparation.	The American Homecoming Act allows Vietnam-born children with American fathers to legally immigrate to the United States.

dream of working your way to the top is alive and well in America but added that she had to work twice as hard as her male counterparts to get there.

During her 2005 commencement speech to Columbia University Business School, Nooyi encouraged graduates to put America's best foot forward in the global marketplace by being culturally sensitive: "As you travel throughout the world to assure America's continued global economic leadership, . . . remember to do your part to influence perception. If you exhibit emotional intelligence as well as academic intelligence, if you ascribe positive intent to all your actions on the international business stage, this can be a great advantage. But if you stomp around in a tone-deaf [cultural] fog, . . . it will also get you in trouble. And when it does, you will have only yourself to blame."

Elaine Chao

Taiwanese native Elaine L. Chao became the first Asian American woman to be appointed to the federal cabinet, becoming the nation's twenty-fourth secretary of labor in 2001. In her post, Chao became the person whom President George W. Bush entrusted with his administration's vi-

1990	1993	1996	1997
In the last thirty years, the U.S. Asian/Pacific Islander population has grown from 1 million to more than 7 million.	Following a thirty-six-day hunger strike by Asian American students, the administration at the University of California agrees to establish an Asian American studies program.	Gary Locke is elected governor of the state of Washington he is the first Asian to hold such a post on the U.S. mainland.	Tiger Woods, whose mother is Thai and father African American, wins the coveted Masters Tournament title en route to becoming the top golfer in the world for most of the next decade.

sion of America in the global workforce. She studied at Harvard, MIT, Dartmouth, and Columbia.

Previously, Chao had been the first Asian American to serve as director of the Peace Corps. She also served for four years as president of the United Way. From 1996 until her appointment as secretary of labor, Chao was a Distinguished Fellow with the Heritage Foundation, a conservative Washington think tank.

Notable Others

Asian American Pulitzer Prize winners have included Huynh Cong Ut, a Vietnamese American, who won the prestigious award in 1972 for photography after being wounded three times while working in the Vietnam War as a photographer. His most memorable work is the haunting photo of a young, naked Vietnamese girl fleeing from a napalm attack. Dr. David Ho, who pioneered the use of the drug "cocktail" that fights HIV/AIDS, was the subject of a Pulitzer-winning series of medical stories. Ho was named *Time* magazine's Man of the Year in 1996 and awarded a Presidential Medal in 2001 for research that helped reduce U.S. and European AIDS deaths to one-fifth of their peak number.

Olympic ice skaters Kristi Yamaguchi and Michelle Kwan, Senator

2000

A total of eight Asian Pacific Americans serve in the 107th Congress, including Daniel Inouye (D-Hawaii), Daniel Akaka (D-Hawaii), Mike Honda (D-California), Patsy Mink (D-Hawaii), Eni Faleomavaega (D-Am Samoa), Robert Matsui (D-California), Robert Underwood (D-Guam) and David Wu (D-Oregon).

2000–2001

Norman Y. Mineta is confirmed as the U.S. secretary of commerce during the final six months of the Clinton administration, making him the first Asian American cabinet member in U.S. history. Mineta is confirmed as the U.S. secretary of transportation in the George W. Bush administration in 2001, the only Democrat in the Bush Cabinet.

Daniel K. Akaka, and newswoman Connie Chung also stand out as hugely successful role models who have bucked career stereotypes.

Astronaut Ellison S. Onizuka, who was killed in the *Challenger* explosion in 1986, and tenacious Houston Rockets center and recent Chinese immigrant Yao Ming have emerged as other notable heroes.

However, many Asian characters in the entertainment realm continue to remain stereotypical figures, such as the indestructible "mystic fighter," introduced by Bruce Lee, and the "China doll," who is subservient and demure and often a sexual toy. Those stereotypes have been puzzlingly slow to vanish. But actors such as Chow Yun-Fat, Michelle Yeoh, and Jackie Chan have all transcended those roles in recent years, as has the popular Hong Kong movie director John Woo.

The 2000 census shows that 10.2 million Americans reported themselves as ethnically wholly Asian and 11.9 million people reported themselves as Asian and at least one other race, data suggesting that 3.6 to 4.2 percent of the U.S. population is of Asian descent. While still a relatively small percentage of the American population, Asian Americans are the most diverse racial/ethnic group in America in terms of language, religion, and customs.

They also continue to wield economic clout. Asian American buy-

2001	2002
Elaine Chao is confirmed as the nation's twenty-fourth secretary of labor and the first Asian American woman appointed to a cabinet post in U.S. history.	The National Asian Pacific American Legal Consortium's *Backlash: When America Turned on Its Own* chronicles a significant spike in racial violence against Asian Americans since the events of 9/11. People who vaguely resemble the enemy, including Sikh Americans and South Asian Americans, have been locked away without due process, the organization charges.

Sources: web.mit.edu; PBS, Ancestors in the Americas, *www.pbs.org/ancestorsintheamericas/timeline.html;* US Asians, *us_asians.tripod.com.*

ing power, which was $344 billion in 2003, should reach $526 billion in 2008, according to the Selig Center at the University of Georgia. In 2003, Asian Americans accounted for 4.2 percent of the country's buying power, up from 2.8 percent in 1990.

In our multiethnic culture, distortion about one group's ethnicity is often the flip side of distortions about another group's ethnicity. For instance, the notion that one ethnic group is "quiet" or "vanilla" might be the converse to the notion that another group is "exotic" or "foreign-looking." Hence, an important part of unlearning racism is the discovery of factual information about a cultural and ethnic heritage. When you perceive people as "foreigners" based only on their looks, you are quietly labeling them nonentities in the American democratic process. When you welcome all people of difference, you are welcoming their valuable contribution into the cultural montage, and everyone benefits from the transformation.

Discussion Questions

1. How can seemingly positive labels and generalizations negatively impact an ethnic population?

2. What modern-day U.S. detention facility has been compared by some in the Asian community to World War II Japanese internment camps?

3. How do America's television and cinema cultures represent the Asian American population?

EIGHT

Arab Americans

A label is easy to stick on but difficult to remove.

—PROVERB

Imagine the plight of Arab Americans post–September 11. After the terrorist attacks, nearly all Arabs and Muslims in the United States were faced with the dual pain of mourning a brutal assault on their countrymen and suddenly having to defend themselves, their families, their culture, and their status as Americans.

Countless Arab Americans quickly found themselves targets for senseless domestic reprisals. Mosques, Arab community centers, and Arab-owned businesses were vandalized. Women and girls wearing the traditional Muslim head covering were harassed and assaulted, vitriolic mail flowed, death threats were leveled, and hate crimes—some of them lethal—flourished. Already suffering under numerous stereotypes, many Arab Americans found themselves harshly relabeled.

Ironically, Arab Americans pitched in as much as any other ethnic population to aid victims with medical help, prayer vigils, blood drives, fund-raisers, and the like. It became painfully apparent to most of this population that the terrorists who committed this diabolical act were no more representative of Muslim and Arab people than Oklahoma City bomber Timothy McVeigh was of Christians and whites. Yet the 2 percent of Americans who practice the Muslim faith continue to feel the sting of an unfair association.

It's not the first time in this country that a group has been hysterically singled out for blame. Jews have been unfairly held responsible for alleged exploitive business practices, gay men for the AIDS epidemic, Italian Americans for organized crime, and Japanese Americans for the Pearl Harbor bombings.

LABELS

Unfortunately, more inappropriate terms and labels for Arab Americans have crept into the national lexicon since the September 11 attacks. Calling any Middle Eastern–looking person an *Osama*—after Osama bin Laden—is very offensive. Another inappropriate term for an Arab American, *Abba Dabba,* was popularized in the movie *Betrayed.* The dehumanizing word *hajji,* often applied to any Iraqi or Middle Easterner, has been commonly used by U.S. occupation forces in both Iraq and Afghanistan. One soldier wrote "Hodgie killer" on his footlocker (Newsobserver.com, 2004).

> *NEVER:* Osama, hajji, raghead, camel jockey, sand monkey, Ayrab, ninja

> *BE CAREFUL WITH:* Arab *and* Muslim *(as general references to all Arab Americans),* Islamic terrorist

> *BEST:* Arab American, *or a specific ethnicity:* Palestinian American, Lebanese American *etc.*

Raghead and *towelhead* are older ethnic slurs designating a male who wears a turban. Terms such as *ninja,* referring to a Muslim woman, and the trite and demeaning *camel jockey, sand monkey* or *sand nigger,* and even *turban cowboy* are, of course, uniformly offensive. *Ay-rab* and *Ahab* remain verbal slurs. Use of the term *patel,* sometimes a derogatory name for an Indian American, is to be avoided except as a person's actual name.

The term *Arab American* or more geographically specific terms such as *Palestinian American* or *Lebanese American* are acceptable and preferred.

Additionally, lumping all Arab terrorists into the category of "Islamic terrorists," just because some of the criminal radicals claim to be speaking for all of Islam, is no more appropriate than calling other anarchists Christian terrorists, Irish terrorists, or Jewish terrorists.

"Slipping the term Islamic on a terrorist if he claims to be fighting under the banner of Islam means you have empowered the terrorist to the level of spokesman for the religion of Islam and attributed his actions to the religion of Islam," wrote Mohamed Elibiary, president of the Freedom and Justice Foundation in Plano, Texas (*Dallas Morning News,* July 2005). "We're only legitimizing our enemy, insulting the faith's practitioners, and disenfranchising our own Western Muslim youth."

Virtually all major Islamic organizations and clerics have condemned the actions of Osama bin Laden's militant fringe. Yet Islam is being blamed for all the terrorism we've read about or experienced in the United States, England, and elsewhere since September 11. True, it is much easier for some Americans to demonize Islam, the Quran, and the Prophet Muhammad as the root of the violence than it is to carefully examine the facts. But such attitudes will not help enhance our country's recently tarnished image overseas, especially among the millions of Islamic followers, or lessen the potential for backlash and hate crimes against our own citizens.

The percentage of Americans who believe that Islam is likely to encourage terrorism has doubled to 46 percent in 2005 since 9/11, a Pew Research survey showed.

CHALLENGES

Going back to a post-9/11 survey commissioned by the Arab American Institute Foundation, we saw that nearly one in five Arab Americans had personally been discriminated against because of their ethnicity soon after the attacks. However, a full 40 percent said they knew someone of Arab ethnicity who has experienced discrimination since the tragedy.

The image of Arab Americans as "billionaires, bombers, and belly dancers" has only been fortified in many people's minds by recent events. But stereotypes of Arab Americans were already prevalent in this country well before the events of recent years. Western images depicting Arabs as sheiks, white-slave owners, and harem dwellers, and as mythical or historical figures such as Ali Baba, the thief of Baghdad, and Sinbad are still amazingly common. Arabs in movies or on TV are often foolish or villainous or both. For example, they're seen as abductors of children in one movie and chief financial backers of espionage in another.

Arab American Timeline

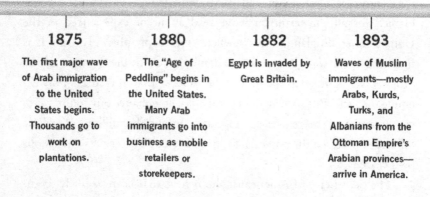

1875	1880	1882	1893
The first major wave of Arab immigration to the United States begins. Thousands go to work on plantations.	The "Age of Peddling" begins in the United States. Many Arab immigrants go into business as mobile retailers or storekeepers.	Egypt is invaded by Great Britain.	Waves of Muslim immigrants—mostly Arabs, Kurds, Turks, and Albanians from the Ottoman Empire's Arabian provinces—arrive in America.

After the FBI's 1978 ABSCAM investigation, in which agents posed as "sheiks" to entrap members of Congress to take bribes, the FBI was criticized for perpetuating stereotypes. (Only a small number of Arab nations actually have sheiks.) Unfortunately, the war in Iraq and the Israel-Palestine conflict only contribute to the emotionally charged notion that all Arabs are enemies of the United States.

Sometimes we create self-fulfilling stereotypes of other people through our actions. Given the nature of the war in Iraq, it is not a stretch to imagine how a soldier there could come to harbor negative expectations of the Iraqi people, believing they were untrustworthy and extremely aggressive, with questionable motives, and treat them in abusive ways as a result—perhaps abusing them verbally or physically or embarrassing them in public. In turn, the Iraqi may easily come to believe that such treatment is typical of Americans and react defensively with heightened hostility toward the soldier, thus "confirming" the American soldier's initial assumption. In the end, both of those assumptions were independent of the real-life traits of both the Iraqi and the soldier.

It's often said that popular culture is a way of having others under-

1907	1915	1919	1920
A case against an American judge who had denied citizenship to a Syrian is won by Syrians. The judge had claimed the man belonged to the "yellow race."	British and Arabs sign the Husayn-McMahon Correspondence, which promises Arabs an independent Arab nation after the world war, composed of the present-day countries of Israel, Syria, Jordan, Saudi Arabia, and Palestine.	The French and British divide up the Arab world in the Sykes-Picot Agreement, contrary to the 1915 British accord. The move spurs additional migration to the United States.	The wave of Arab immigration to the United States slows as immigration laws are tightened.

stand you. However, unchallenged stereotypes create a vacuum and only serve to accomplish the opposite. At a time when the Arab American community—which now numbers over 3 million—most needs to feel a sense of belonging and a boost of confidence, these labels continue to isolate them.

It doesn't help that the U.S. government, in its zeal to root out the terrorists and their associates, rounded up and arrested hundreds of Muslims, Arabs, and Arab Americans, many of whom were innocent of any crime. Yet they were still picked up, often physically abused, and held incommunicado indefinitely, in a response that many called racial profiling. Several survivors of the Japanese internment camps during World War II said they couldn't help but shudder at their own memories of detainment and loss of due process, which they compared to the Guantánamo Bay detention facility and the secret prisons where captives were held.

Because the United States remains in a state of war against terrorism, there has been a tendency to reduce the "enemy" to a uniformly mocked and hated figure. Though often wrongly depicted as being less than civil

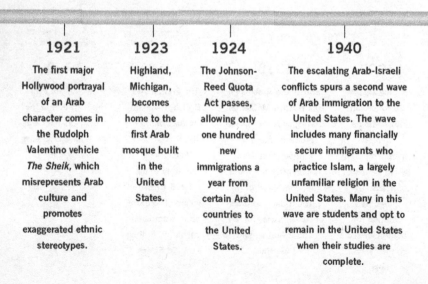

1921

The first major Hollywood portrayal of an Arab character comes in the Rudolph Valentino vehicle *The Sheik*, which misrepresents Arab culture and promotes exaggerated ethnic stereotypes.

1923

Highland, Michigan, becomes home to the first Arab mosque built in the United States.

1924

The Johnson-Reed Quota Act passes, allowing only one hundred new immigrations a year from certain Arab countries to the United States.

1940

The escalating Arab-Israeli conflicts spurs a second wave of Arab immigration to the United States. The wave includes many financially secure immigrants who practice Islam, a largely unfamiliar religion in the United States. Many in this wave are students and opt to remain in the United States when their studies are complete.

or as working menial jobs, the percentage of Arab Americans who attend college is actually higher than the national average. Compared to the norm, about twice as many Arab Americans earn degrees beyond a bachelor's. About 60 percent of working Arab Americans are executives, professionals, or office and sales staff (*Detroit Free Press*, "100 Questions and Answers about Arab-Americans," 2001).

LEADERS

Donna Shalala

Donna Shalala, of Lebanese descent, became the first Arab American appointed to a cabinet secretary post when she was named secretary of the Department of Health and Human Services under the Clinton administration; she served from 1993 to 2000. With her steadfast dedication to education and public service, which included a stint in Iran with the Peace Corps, Shalala has served as a leader and role model her entire life.

1944	1947	1950	1956
The American destroyer escort USS *Naifeh* is named in honor of an Arab-American hero, Navy lieutenant Alfred Naifeh of Oklahoma.	Palestine is split into an Arab state and a Jewish state by the newly formed United Nations.	Ralph Bunche is awarded the Nobel Peace Prize for his work as United Nations mediator in the Arab-Israeli dispute in Palestine.	Israel, Britain, and France invade Egypt when Egypt takes over the Suez Canal, previously controlled by Britain and France.

Shalala, now president of the University of Miami, spent nine years earlier, in her career teaching political science at Bernard Baruch College and Columbia Teachers College. In 1975, while still teaching, she became the director and treasurer of New York City's Municipal Assistance Corporation, helping lift the city out of near financial collapse. The *Washington Post* has said that she is "one of the most successful managers in modern times," while *Business Week* named her "one of the top five managers in higher education."

Shalala also served under President Carter as assistant secretary for policy research and development at the Department of Housing and Urban Development (HUD), where she helped promote antidiscrimination legislation, established women's shelters, and created mortgage credits for women.

As head of the University of Miami, a private school with fourteen thousand students and four campuses, Shalala is devoted to fighting the threat posed by narrow-minded outlooks on the world, a commitment she calls "the pursuit of excellence in the way we treat each other" (Arab-American Business, 2001).

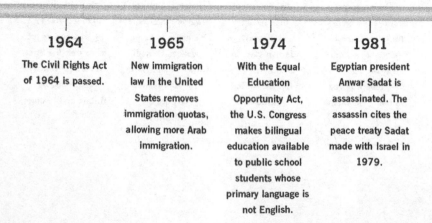

1964	1965	1974	1981
The Civil Rights Act of 1964 is passed.	New immigration law in the United States removes immigration quotas, allowing more Arab immigration.	With the Equal Education Opportunity Act, the U.S. Congress makes bilingual education available to public school students whose primary language is not English.	Egyptian president Anwar Sadat is assassinated. The assassin cites the peace treaty Sadat made with Israel in 1979.

Ray Hanania

Chicago native Ray Hanania, an award-winning journalist, columnist, Pulitzer Prize nominee, author, and stand-up comedian, serves as an important voice of reflection and moderation for the U.S. Arab community. Currently, he is the only Palestinian American journalist whose columns are nationally syndicated.

The author of such books as *The Moral Jihad: Defining the Moderate Palestinian Voice in the Battle against Extremism* and the humorous *I'm Glad I Look like a Terrorist: Growing Up Arab in America,* Hanania (hanania.com, 2005) says he launched his public comedy performances after 9/11 to help cut through the irrational animosity leveled at the Arab American community. He is also managing editor of the popular Web page TheArabStreet.Com.

A Christian Palestinian with a Jewish wife, Hanania was elected on a platform of peace as the national president of the Palestinian American Congress. He attended the 1993 White House peace signing between Yitzhak Rabin and Yasir Arafat and participated in numerous meetings with President Clinton, Arafat, and officials of the Palestinian and Israeli Labor governments.

1987	1988	1990–91	1996
The U.S. Supreme court acknowledges protecting Arab Americans under existing U.S. civil rights legislation.	George Mitchell, an Arab American, becomes U.S. Senate majority leader.	Iraq invades Kuwait. A U.S.-led military coalition launches the Gulf War in 1991 and defeats Saddam Hussein's Iraqi forces but does not capture Hussein. Many Kuwaits, Iraqis, and Palestinians flee to America.	Ralph Nader, an Arab American, runs for U.S. president as the nominee of the environmentally conscious Green Party.

Hanania has noted on his Web site that Arab Americans "have been taking a beating especially in the American media since time immemorial in this country. . . . This started before and has continued after Sept. 11th. The only difference today is that the criticism occurs more frequently. No profiles of prominent Arab-Americans [appear in the mainstream media]. No Arab-American role models are showcased. There are fewer than sixty Arab Americans who work in the mainstream media. In Chicago, where I live, Arabs have been a part of this city's history for more than 125 years. Yet, we don't have one street, one building, one monument, one statue, one holiday or one festival honoring our many contributions to the city."

Notable Others

Our country has numerous high-profile Arab American business leaders. They include Ray R. Irani, CEO of Occidental Petroleum, former Ford Motor Company president Jacques Nasser, and Kinko's founder Paul Orfalea.

Orfalea, whose curly hair spurred him to name the company (now FedEx Kinko's), espoused a unique freethinking and creative business philosophy and passion for retail that have since been emulated widely.

1999	1999	2000
Jordan's King Hussein, the longest reigning Arab ruler, dies.	The Kahlil Gibran Spirit of Humanity Award is launched to recognize individuals, corporations, organizations, and communities whose work and support make a difference in promoting coexistence and inclusion in all walks of life.	Ralph Nader's second presidential run impacts the controversial 2000 election.

After leaving the company, he formed the Orfalea Family Foundation, a philanthropic group focusing on early-care child and infant centers. He is also creating additional public awareness of early-care needs for children of working parents and has worked with government and business leaders to help provide this benefit to children and their families.

Other prominent Arab American leaders include pioneering heart surgeon Dr. Michael DeBakey, whose invention of the miniature ventricular-assist device won him NASA's esteemed Commercial Invention of the Year honors. The hugely successful device is used as an effective long-term "bridge" to a future transplant.

Spencer Abraham, who was sworn in as the tenth secretary of energy on January 20, 2001, is Arab American, and two winners of the Nobel Prize for Chemistry, Dr. Ahmed H. Zewail, a professor of physics at the California Institute of Technology, and Harvard's Dr. Elias Corey, are as well.

Actor Jamie Farr, the late entertainer Danny Thomas, NFL quarterback Doug Flutie, the late iconoclastic rocker Frank Zappa, Herbert "Tiny Tim" Khaury, feisty White House beat journalist Helen Thomas, singer Paul Anka, and broadcaster Casey Kasem are just a few other distinguished Arab Americans in the media and entertainment fields.

2001	2002	2003
On September 11, the World Trade Center complex and the Pentagon are attacked by Muslim jihadists who hijacked commercial airliners and used them as weapons. Many innocent Arab Americans are harassed, assaulted, and arrested without due cause in the aftermath.	The UN passes a Security Council resolution demanding unfettered access for UN inspectors to search for weapons of mass destruction in Iraq.	The United States launches a war against Iraq. No weapons of mass destruction are found. War becomes a divisive force in American politics and society.

CHALLENGES

Challenges ahead for the Arab American community include finding ways to put its best feet forward amid all the disinformation and stereotyping. The new Arab American Museum in Dearborn, Michigan, is a shining example of the possibilities. Finding ways to put more members into the media to ensure that an accurate version of events is presented is another attainable objective. One of the problems in perception is that parts of the Arab community come from societies where journalism and criticism of the government don't exist.

Some argue that the media already gives Arab Americans ample and fair coverage. Of course, that's true only if the news reports of Middle East violence and terrorism are included, say Arab American leaders. The biggest concern of Arab Americans is the feeling that they are being discriminated against because of the perception that terrorists are only Arabs. All but a tiny minority of the Arab American community is still feeling the backlash from incidents of terrorism and hostage taking that in no way involved them.

Casting a net over an entire race based on the actions of a few only heightens the potential for backlash and discrimination. It only serves to dis-

2004

The Palestinian leader Yasir Arafat dies.

2005–2006

As the Iraq War continues, the U.S. prisoners-of-war camp at Guantánamo Bay in Cuba draws strong worldwide criticism for detainment of Arab and Muslim prisoners without trial and for alleged torture. Its detainees are considered by the United States to be illegal combatants who are not entitled to the protections of the Geneva Convention.

Sources: University of Michigan–Ann Arbor, Malouma Study Guide, www.ums.org/pdfs/studyguide/malouma-sg.pdf.

enfranchise several million productive American citizens who have much to offer our culture. By transcending the temptation to label all Arab Americans, you transform yourself into a wiser and more compassionate human being.

Discussion Questions

1. Can you think of a time when you or members of your peer group were blamed for an act or incident in which you were not involved? What was your reaction?

2. Since 9/11, which stereotypes about Muslims and Arab American have been most prevalent? What about before 9/11?

3. After the Oklahoma City bombings of 1995, what group or groups came under immediate suspicion? Who were the actual perpetrators?

A Resilient Population Stares Down Its Labelers

While we know that the dozens of diverse faiths that make up our world mosaic have been regular targets of distrust, discrimination, and scorn throughout history, we've chosen to keep our focus more on ethnic populations and cultures in this book.

But the Jewish community, which in many ways embodies the melding of culture and faith in our world, has consistently fallen prey to labels, programming, and irrational violence from the early ages of recorded human history. Today the Jewish community remains at the emotional epicenter of world events and continues to be subject to misunderstandings and misinterpretations in the United States as well.

Slowly vanishing are such labels as *Christ killer, Heeb, hymie, Hooknose, Kike, Yid,* and economic stereotypes such as *penny chaser,* as well as jokes and references to the murderous tools of the Holocaust. But their use is stubbornly clung to in some circles, despite their shockingly cruel and offensive nature and the inhumanity wrought upon the Jewish population.

Similarly, public skepticism still exists among some international political leaders and extremists that the World War II–era Jewish genocide ever happened, despite overwhelming telling evidence that death-camp extermination and other violence killed about 5.5 million Jews, or roughly half of Europe's Jewish population, the highest percentage of any people who fell victim to the war.

Even when faced with discrimination and prejudice, the Jewish community has always responded by creating peaceful organizations that have fought for acceptance and tolerance.

In the United States, where millions of Eastern European Jews fled between 1880 and 1924 to escape persecution and other hardships, the Jewish community organized networks to "Americanize" and settle the new immigrants. That immigration push, followed by a second wave of Jews fleeing the horrors of the Holocaust in the late 1930s and early 1940s, made America home to the largest Jewish population in the world.

While anti-Semitism has been less insidious in America than in many other countries, it was common and even normalized here before World War II. Xenophobia resulted in only minimal violence in the United States, but draconian restrictions on Jewish immigration abounded, as did widespread discrimination in employment and social circles. Access to clubs, resorts, colleges, and teaching positions was also limited, as was access to mortgage lending outside of certain "redlined" neighborhoods populated predominantly by Jews. Jewish businesses were sometimes targeted for looting or even burning.

Anti-Semitism reached its zenith in the United States with the rise of the Ku Klux Klan and virulent anti-Semitic speeches of several high-profile individuals, including religious leaders and business leaders.

Today turmoil in the Middle East, ongoing disputes over parts of the Holy Land, plus Israel's political and strategic affiliations with the United States, continue to spawn ill-aimed animosity for Jews in many parts of the world.

Some believe that the Jewish population's ability to quickly assimilate into a society has aroused more enmity than a tendency toward separateness would. "He does indeed become a native, quite indistinguishable as a stranger by any sign whatever," writes Rabbi Adin Steinsaltz in his book *We Jews: Who Are We and What Should We Do.* "And this is what causes fierce antagonism among many people.

(cont.)

(cont.)

They fear that this stranger has taken their very essence from them. Moreover, the personal enmity becomes a much more general hatred when this Jew ceases to be a particular individual in one's circle and becomes a public image" such as a writer, film star, statesman, or military commander.

But the labels and strife endured by American Jews didn't keep Jewish composer Irving Berlin, who emigrated from Siberia in 1893, from writing "God Bless America" in gratitude for what he said was the wealth of opportunities that America gave him.

Though the Jewish people have endured centuries of racial, religious, and ethnic strife, their resilience in overcoming the obstacles and pogroms of their history stands as an example of leadership beyond labels. The Jewish population continues to show that personal leadership is key in preserving a culture and continuing noteworthy social, educational, and economic contributions.

NINE

Gender Wars: Women

> Nobody objects to a woman being a good writer or sculptor or geneticist if at the same time she manages to be a good wife, a good mother, good-looking, good-tempered, well-dressed, well-groomed, and unaggressive.
>
> —MARYA MANNES

Making up more than half of the population, women are certainly not a "minority" by strict definition. The Census Bureau predicts that women will continue to outnumber men throughout the first half of this century, going from a numerical difference of 5.3 million in 2000 to 6.9 million in 2050. But even a cursory look at the past reveals an epic struggle casting our adult female population in an uphill fight for rights that is now considered one of the longest and toughest human rights struggles in United States history.

It is telling that the century-and-half-long campaign for the most basic democratic privilege came to fruition only eighty-six years ago, when the Nineteenth Amendment, guaranteeing that "the right of citizens of the United States to vote shall not be denied or abridged by the United States or by any State on account of sex," was ratified.

While we've come a long way since the suffrage movement, equal footing for both sexes is still somewhat elusive at home and abroad. It doesn't help that much of our world, including the American culture, has treated women as second-class citizens since the beginning of recorded time. Even with obvious progress, this population group is still in a catch-up mode with the country's status quo, much like our nation's minority groups.

Through the centuries, women have been portrayed not only as intellectually inferior to men but as a major source of evil and temptation. In Greek mythology, for example, it was a woman, Pandora, who opened the forbidden box and brought unhappiness and plagues to the world.

Although changes in the U.S. culture and economic structure have freed women for roles other than marriage and motherhood in the last three or four generations, societal pressures still keep many talented women from finishing college or progressing fairly through their careers of choice.

It's not that progress in removing societal labels hasn't been significant in the past few decades. However, we are still seeing many of the old fixed media images reinforced: the femme fatale, the sex kitten, the "emasculating" corporate climber, and the ubiquitous American super-woman/supermom, who tries to be all things to everyone.

Many women are still compelled to judge themselves by the standards of a male-dominated workplace and the multibillion-dollar beauty industry. This "cult of perfection," a product of Madison Avenue, seems to demand thinness and 24/7 glamour, and it continues to envelop and preoccupy many women, either consciously or subconsciously. Some readers may remember the old perfume advertisement, where a woman belts out, "I can bring home the bacon, fry it up in a pan. And never let you forget you're a man . . ." We still put intense pressure on women.

While women make up more than 50 percent of the population, in 2005 they only represented 14 percent of our highest legislative body, the

U.S. Senate. There have been no women presidents—yet. There's been but one woman vice presidential candidate, Geraldine Ferraro, in 1984. Of course, the political complexion is always subject to change.

Politics aside, how many female business leaders, filmmakers, famous scientists, or foreign heads of state can most people name? There are a few more now than there were a decade or two ago, but not many. These remain male-dominated professions in a male-dominated world.

Women professionals and women athletes also continue to get short shrift in news coverage. Several studies show that less than 20 percent of network airtime in sports and news programs is dedicated to women.

And in the all-important paycheck category, women are expected to earn about eighty cents for every dollar their male counterparts make this year, say the latest studies and estimates from the General Accounting Office (GAO). This pay gap has lingered for the past two decades, even when all work-related and demographic factors such as race, industry, occupation, marital status, and job tenure are factored in.

Data also suggest that working women are still penalized for their dual roles as wage earner and homemaker-caregiver. Women in the labor force are less able to work a full-time schedule and more likely to leave the workforce for longer spans than men, stifling women's earnings even further. Working women who have children earn 2.5 percent less than women without them, while men with children earn 2 percent more than men without children. In other words, women lose some traction in the workplace because many employers fear they'll be perennially tempted by the "mommy track."

Yet companies with the best representation of women in their management ranks also return the greatest value to shareholders and post the strongest return on equity, according to a study by Catalyst, a leading research and advisory organization on women's issues.

Attrition cost American companies $11 billion last year, and a large portion of that turnover can be attributed to women leaving jobs where their talents had not been cultivated and their contributions were not appreciated. That is not to say that women have it better in business cultures in other parts of the world. By some estimates, women work close to two-thirds of the world's work hours but earn only one-tenth of the world's income.

Despite more-than-ample challenges, women continue to claim or reclaim more personal and professional freedoms every day. The Center for Women's Business Research estimates that as of 2004, nearly half of all privately held businesses in the United States were owned 50 percent or more by women, including 6.7 million firms that were majority-owned by women and another 4 million firms owned equally by women and men. The center also estimates that women-owned firms employ more than 19 million people in the United States—or one in seven of all employees. These vital—and viable—business owners fuel the economy through production of necessary goods and services and the contribution of billions in purchasing power.

Industry is talent-driven today, not gender- or race-driven. What matters now is if a person has the skills and leadership ability to get the job done. Whether the "glass ceiling" for women is self-inflicted by low

Women's Rights Timeline

1701	1769	1776
Albany, New York, becomes the site of the first sexually integrated jury to hear cases.	The American colonies elect to base some laws on English common law, which had been summarized as follows: "The very being and legal existence of the woman is suspended during the marriage, or at least is incorporated into that of her husband under whose wing and protection she performs everything."	U.S. president John Adams, in response to his wife, Abigail, who pleads with him to "remember the ladies" in new and revised laws, replies that men will strongly oppose the "despotism of the petticoat."

self-esteem and cultural tradition or merely reflects someone's inability to recognize talent and leadership, it can be cracked. Prospering women have the opportunity and the ability to help others develop a sense of identity, direction, and control and to serve as transformational figures.

Today the power is in the hands of each individual woman to supersede her circumstances by reevaluating the situation, recognizing the possibilities, affirming her worth, and determining how to create opportunities and capitalize on them.

More women leaders are needed in business to broaden perspectives, break down barriers, and effect positive change inside and outside corporate America. It is simply good business. If good leaders fail to make the most of the business potential or any of their people, they limit the company's productivity and growth.

For women to transcend gender perceptions and the added complexities of balancing family and career, they need to create a personal "brand" that propels them forward in their career path or the marketplace. Creating this success brand, and identifying and addressing habits and patterns that interfere with success, can result in transformation, which knows no boundaries of gender, labels, or class.

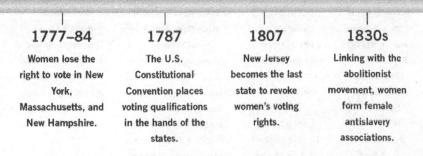

1777–84	1787	1807	1830s
Women lose the right to vote in New York, Massachusetts, and New Hampshire.	The U.S. Constitutional Convention places voting qualifications in the hands of the states.	New Jersey becomes the last state to revoke women's voting rights.	Linking with the abolitionist movement, women form female antislavery associations.

LABELS AND GENDER CODING

We've shown how labels, stereotypes, and social judgments are commonly used to perpetuate inequities in our system. But a less conspicuous means of subjugation can occur in everyday language. The English language, despite all its evolutions, remains gender-coded and, to a degree, gender-biased.

For example, use of the pronoun *he* when a person means "he or she" is just one of many built-in codes. Although the word *man* originally had a dual meaning of "adult human" and "adult male," its definition has evolved over the years to be more closely identified with the male, thus its generic use should be avoided if possible, says a primer on nonsexist language use from the Writing Lab at Purdue University.

Gender bias is not as hard to avoid as you might think. For example, you can use *humanity* instead of *mankind, human achievement* instead of *mankind's achievement* and *staff hours* instead of *man hours*. The same goes with words that assume the sex of a person, such as *salesman, chair-*

1839	1840	1848	1855
Mississippi becomes the first state to grant women the right to hold property in their own names but stipulates that they must have the permission of their husbands.	Elizabeth Cady Stanton, Lucretia Mott, and other women are barred from participating in the World Anti-Slavery Convention in London because of their gender.	The first women's rights convention is held in Seneca Falls, New York. Equal suffrage is proposed by Elizabeth Cady Stanton. Three hundred women and men sign a Declaration of Sentiments, a plea for the end of discrimination against women in society.	A Missouri black slave woman is declared to be property and told she has no right to defend herself against her master's sexual assault in the case *Missouri v. Celia.*

man, housewife, and *fireman.* The terms *salesperson, chairperson* (or just *chair*), *homemaker,* and *firefighter* are equally effective replacements.

Some call this just another push for "political correctness." The truth is, our language is in a constant state of evolution and heading in a less sexist direction. Though you probably won't be held up to scorn if you use some gender-coded terminology, why hang on to something that is obsolete, inaccurate, and even disrespectful? Business and social leaders are quickly grasping this reality faster than others and moving forward with it.

Overgeneralizations are probably worse than sexist language. You have heard them: women are weak by nature, submissive, clumsy, bad drivers, dependent, overly emotional, and indecisive. Such characterizations imply that men are customarily the polar opposite. That the two sexes have different traits is obvious. But should women be lumped into a category with an expectation that they conform to these overgeneralizations?

The good news? As more women gain influence behind the scenes in

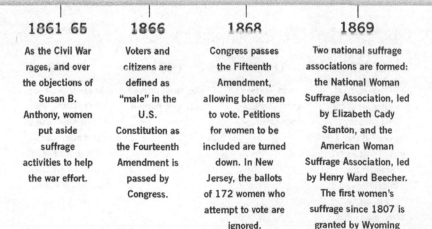

1861 65	1866	1868	1869
As the Civil War rages, and over the objections of Susan B. Anthony, women put aside suffrage activities to help the war effort.	Voters and citizens are defined as "male" in the U.S. Constitution as the Fourteenth Amendment is passed by Congress.	Congress passes the Fifteenth Amendment, allowing black men to vote. Petitions for women to be included are turned down. In New Jersey, the ballots of 172 women who attempt to vote are ignored.	Two national suffrage associations are formed: the National Woman Suffrage Association, led by Elizabeth Cady Stanton, and the American Woman Suffrage Association, led by Henry Ward Beecher. The first women's suffrage since 1807 is granted by Wyoming Territory.

the business and political worlds, the decades of negative, exploitive, and inaccurate stereotyping seem to be winding down.

Some derogatory labels, slurs, and images are slow to die, however. And there are quite a few more for women than there are for men. Terms such as *slut, bimbo, shrew, floozy, tramp, battle-ax, gold digger, old broad, bag,* and *dumb blonde,* among many others, remain common, as are a host of sexual slurs that we won't repeat here.

The fact that you hear many of the aforementioned words on network television now—as well as terms such as *booty* and *ho*—only serves to legitimize this vocabulary in mainstream culture.

NEVER: *slut, bimbo, bitch, shrew, floozy, tramp, battle-ax, gold digger, old broad, bag, dumb blonde, whore, honeypot, easy, other sexual innuendos and slang*

BE CAREFUL WITH: *male-biased language, girls*

BEST: *women, ladies*

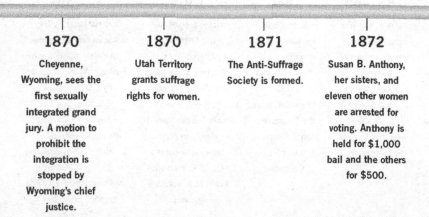

1870

Cheyenne, Wyoming, sees the first sexually integrated grand jury. A motion to prohibit the integration is stopped by Wyoming's chief justice.

1870

Utah Territory grants suffrage rights for women.

1871

The Anti-Suffrage Society is formed.

1872

Susan B. Anthony, her sisters, and eleven other women are arrested for voting. Anthony is held for $1,000 bail and the others for $500.

Derogatory words describing promiscuous behavior are almost exclusively tailored for the female gender: *slut, honeypot, easy.* The rare times when there's a male equivalent, it is usually not as demeaning and can even be heroic or romanticized: *Casanova, stud, stallion.* Meanwhile, women who don't "put out" are "frigid" or "cold." Women often feel as if they are forced to define their sexuality in terms of such polarizing, male-imposed words, a game that seems to cast them further into a second-class citizenship—the role of the male adjunct. Logically, these biases are passed along to our children, who are getting plenty of sexist input when they see the body parts of unclad or scantily clad women used to sell all types of common products.

Girls and women are also bombarded with media advice telling them how to be skinny, how to augment their bodies, and in general, how to change themselves to please everyone else. While women in advertisements are now showing up more frequently behind the wheel of a vehicle than sprawled across its hood scantily clad, they are still seen regularly toiling for cleaners and other household products in stereotypical fashion.

With some resistance, however, women have become increasingly

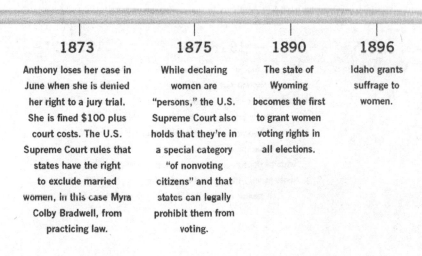

1873	1875	1890	1896
Anthony loses her case in June when she is denied her right to a jury trial. She is fined $100 plus court costs. The U.S. Supreme Court rules that states have the right to exclude married women, in this case Myra Colby Bradwell, from practicing law.	While declaring women are "persons," the U.S. Supreme Court also holds that they're in a special category "of nonvoting citizens" and that states can legally prohibit them from voting.	The state of Wyoming becomes the first to grant women voting rights in all elections.	Idaho grants suffrage to women.

competitive in traditional male sports strongholds. Danica Patrick has excelled in auto racing and LPGA greats Annika Sorenstam and Michelle Wie have participated in several men's PGA golf tour events—performances that are helping propel more female athletes into the limelight, while calling additional attention to women's professional sports.

LEADERS

To be a female role model in this country in the early 1800s was a monumental challenge and an act of almost unprecedented courage. Society demanded that women of that era be seen and not heard.

Elizabeth Cady Stanton

Elizabeth Cady Stanton, who was among the first women to fight for equality on a national scale, overcame huge hurdles in doing so. Born in 1815 in Johnstown, New York, she grew up with a keen understanding of oppression. Her father was an abolitionist and attorney, and she often spoke with runaway slaves who were sheltered at her cousin's home.

1906	1916	1910–11
Susan B. Anthony dies.	Margaret Sanger defies New York's anticontraception law by establishing a Brooklyn clinic. She is among the first of hundreds arrested for the same "offense." Two years later, Sanger wins a U.S. Supreme Court case over the rights of doctors to advise married patients about birth control options for health purposes.	California and the state of Washington grant women voting rights.

She attended Troy Female Seminary, one of the first American educational institutions to provide women with an education comparable to that of men. At the time of the seminary's founding in 1821, women were barred from colleges with the exception of a few academies that offered such "female arts" as embroidery and conversational French.

When Stanton and her husband, fellow abolitionist Henry Stanton, traveled to London to attend the World Anti-Slavery Convention in 1842, they found that convention organizers wouldn't allow women delegates to participate. While there, Stanton met American Lucretia Mott, who was equally enraged at her exclusion, and the two vowed that equality for all women would become an additional priority.

Stanton and Mott would be among the approximately three hundred people of both sexes to sign a document calling for the end of discrimination against women in all levels of society. Called the Declaration of Sentiments, it was modeled after the Declaration of Independence.

Completed at the Seneca Falls Convention of 1848, the declaration demanded that women be afforded the right to vote, to speak freely, to own property, and to hold jobs for the same pay as men. Though scoffed at by the power elite at first, the act was considered a launching point

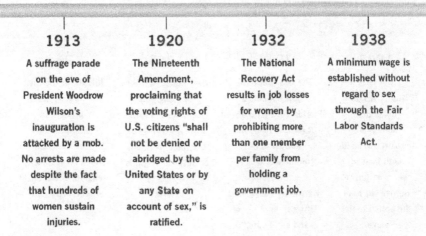

1913	1920	1932	1938
A suffrage parade on the eve of President Woodrow Wilson's inauguration is attacked by a mob. No arrests are made despite the fact that hundreds of women sustain injuries.	The Nineteenth Amendment, proclaiming that the voting rights of U.S. citizens "shall not be denied or abridged by the United States or by any State on account of sex," is ratified.	The National Recovery Act results in job losses for women by prohibiting more than one member per family from holding a government job.	A minimum wage is established without regard to sex through the Fair Labor Standards Act.

for the American women's rights movement. Stanton later founded the American Equal Rights Association with Susan B. Anthony in 1866.

Stanton died in 1902 in New York City, eighteen years before our Constitution would have finally granted her the right to vote. But the dedication of Stanton and others who led this massive human rights movement laid the groundwork for change.

Eleanor Roosevelt

Born in 1884, Eleanor Roosevelt came to be best known for her humanity and compassion. She was often called the "most admired woman in America" and "First Lady of the Western World," tremendous accomplishments for someone who lost both parents at a young age and grew up a shy girl under the watch of an overly protective grandmother.

Eleanor overcame that shyness to become a graceful and self-confident woman with a distinct voice in public affairs and policy, serving as a champion for people of all colors, creeds, and convictions—traits that elicited criticism from some but adoration from most. The wife of Franklin Delano Roosevelt and a mother of six, Eleanor took an activist role as first lady, serving as assistant secretary of the navy and assuming a leadership role in the women's division of the New York State Democra-

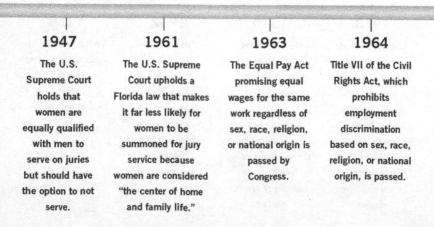

1947	1961	1963	1964
The U.S. Supreme Court holds that women are equally qualified with men to serve on juries but should have the option to not serve.	The U.S. Supreme Court upholds a Florida law that makes it far less likely for women to be summoned for jury service because women are considered "the center of home and family life."	The Equal Pay Act promising equal wages for the same work regardless of sex, race, religion, or national origin is passed by Congress.	Title VII of the Civil Rights Act, which prohibits employment discrimination based on sex, race, religion, or national origin, is passed.

tic Committee. She was a vocal proponent of education for all and made frequent visits to American armed forces abroad during World War II. She ignored precedent by organizing press conferences, lecturing across the country, and delivering her opinions through radio broadcasts and a syndicated newspaper column called "My Day."

After her husband's death in 1945, Roosevelt returned to their Hyde Park home but soon emerged into society and politics again, this time as a U.S. spokesperson in the United Nations, a role she continued in until her death in 1962. Said UN ambassador Adlai Stevenson, "What other single human being has touched and transformed the existence of so many? [Eleanor Roosevelt] walked in the slums and ghettos of the world, not on a tour of inspection, but as one who could not feel contentment when others were hungry."

Hillary Rodham Clinton

A more recent women's rights leader, Senator Hillary Rodham Clinton, is also shaking things up. The New York senator is expected to make a precedent-setting run for her party's presidential nomination in 2008. Clinton emerged as an international advocate for women and girls throughout the world during her eight years as first lady. In her historic

1968	1969	1971
An executive order prohibiting sex discrimination by government contractors is issued.	California becomes the first state to adopt no-fault divorce, allowing divorce by mutual agreement. The U.S. Circuit Court of Appeals rules that women can work in jobs once exclusively held by men if they meet the job's physical requirements.	Practice of employers' refusing to hire mothers with preschool children is outlawed by the U.S. Supreme Court.

speech at the United Nation's International Conference on Women in Beijing in 1995, she said, "If there is one message that echoes forth from this conference, let it be that human rights are women's rights. . . . And women's rights are human rights, once and for all."

Clinton was the lead sponsor of the Paycheck Fairness Act of 2005, designed to strengthen enforcement of equal pay laws. Her work on behalf of Title IX, which has provided equal access to education and sports for young women in our high schools and colleges, was recognized in 2005 with the Presidential Award, presented by the National Association for Girls and Women in Sport.

Clinton has been a strong supporter of the Violence Against Women Act and has worked to ensure adequate resources for the Violence Against Women office in the Department of Justice. She is also a longtime advocate of reproductive freedom for women. She even discovered an unlikely ally in recent years in ex–House speaker and former political foe Newt Gingrich; the two have tried to push through a variety of lifesaving health-care reforms for adoption by the government and private insurers.

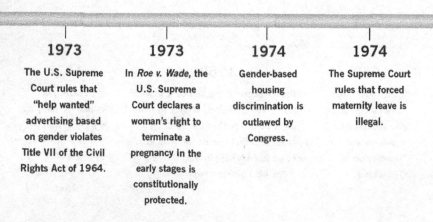

1973	1973	1974	1974
The U.S. Supreme Court rules that "help wanted" advertising based on gender violates Title VII of the Civil Rights Act of 1964.	In *Roe v. Wade*, the U.S. Supreme Court declares a woman's right to terminate a pregnancy in the early stages is constitutionally protected.	Gender-based housing discrimination is outlawed by Congress.	The Supreme Court rules that forced maternity leave is illegal.

Betty Friedan

A forerunner to Clinton, the late Betty Friedan, author and cofounder in 1966 of the National Organization for Women (NOW), dedicated much of her life to achieving equality of opportunity for women. A founding member of the National Women's Political Caucus, Friedan was a leader of the campaign for ratification of the Equal Rights Amendment.

Her landmark and controversial work *The Feminine Mystique* became an immediate best seller when it was published in 1963. Its premise, that women were pawns of a male value system that forced them to live a narrow existence and find fulfillment only through their husbands and children, seemed to strike a responsive chord among American women.

In fact, the book is now considered to be one of the most influential of the last century. Said Friedan, "When she stopped conforming to the conventional picture of femininity, she finally began to enjoy being a woman."

Over the years, both Friedan and Clinton endured slurs from opponents and columnists that male politicians and activists were not subjected to. When Clinton was first lady, she was referred to as a "witch" or

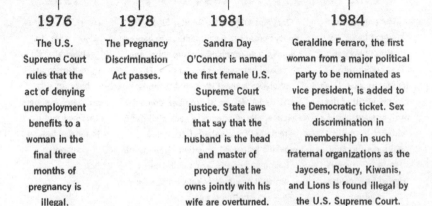

1976	1978	1981	1984
The U.S. Supreme Court rules that the act of denying unemployment benefits to a woman in the final three months of pregnancy is illegal.	The Pregnancy Discrimination Act passes.	Sandra Day O'Connor is named the first female U.S. Supreme Court justice. State laws that say that the husband is the head and master of property that he owns jointly with his wife are overturned.	Geraldine Ferraro, the first woman from a major political party to be nominated as vice president, is added to the Democratic ticket. Sex discrimination in membership in such fraternal organizations as the Jaycees, Rotary, Kiwanis, and Lions is found illegal by the U.S. Supreme Court.

"witchlike" at least fifty times in the press. That record prompted Boston University journalism professor Caryl Rivers, coauthor of *Same Difference: How Gender Myths Are Hurting Our Relationships, Our Children, and Our Jobs,* to write, "Male political figures may be called mean and nasty names, but those words don't usually reflect superstition and dread. Did the press ever call Presidents Carter, Reagan, Bush, or Clinton warlocks?"

Clinton and Friedan have also been characterized as "man haters" and "feminazis" by their mostly white-male opponents.

It is clear that what women first fought for in the suffrage movement—and are still slowly winning—was a reevaluation of their traditional roles at all levels of society. But like other barrier-breaking efforts of the past, the process has been—and still is—a slow one.

Condoleezza Rice

Alabama native Condoleezza Rice has broken down many barriers for women and African Americans. Born November 14, 1954, in Birmingham, Rice rose to epitomize the value of education. She graduated Phi

1993	1994	1997
The Family and Medical Leave Act, which provides workers with temporary work leave in the event of the birth or adoption of a child or the serious health condition of a family member, is signed by President Clinton.	Congress adopts the Gender Equity in Education Act to train teachers in gender equity, teen pregnancy counseling, and sexual harassment prevention. The Violence against Women Act funds services for victims of rape and domestic violence, allows women to seek civil rights remedies for gender-related crimes, provides increased sensitivity training to police and courts, and establishes a national twenty-four-hour hotline for battered women.	The U.S. Supreme Court rules that college athletic programs must have roughly equivalent numbers of women and men to receive federal support.

Beta Kappa from the University of Denver, where she'd later earn her Ph.D. in international studies, after earning a master's at Notre Dame.

Rice was named U.S. secretary of state in January 2005, the first woman to earn that position and the second African American, following Colin Powell. A distinguished academic career preceded her entry into the political fray. Rice served six years as provost for Stanford University, where she was responsible for a $1.5 billion annual budget, 1,400 faculty, and 14,000 students. As a professor of political science, she won two of the highest teaching honors—the 1984 Walter J. Gores Award for Excellence in Teaching and the 1993 School of Humanities and Sciences Dean's Award for Distinguished Teaching.

Rice has also served as director and senior director of Soviet and East European Affairs in the National Security Council, and as special assistant to the president for national security affairs during Germany's reunification and the final days of the Soviet Union, as well as in many other critical posts. Rice was also a member of the Federal Advisory Committee on Gender-Integrated Training for the U.S. Military.

Rice's advice has long been sought by major companies and institu-

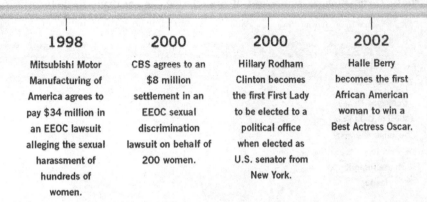

1998	2000	2000	2002
Mitsubishi Motor Manufacturing of America agrees to pay $34 million in an EEOC lawsuit alleging the sexual harassment of hundreds of women.	CBS agrees to an $8 million settlement in an EEOC sexual discrimination lawsuit on behalf of 200 women.	Hillary Rodham Clinton becomes the first First Lady to be elected to a political office when elected as U.S. senator from New York.	Halle Berry becomes the first African American woman to win a Best Actress Oscar.

tions across the country. She's served on the boards of Chevron Corporation, Charles Schwab, the William and Flora Hewlett Foundation, the University of Notre Dame, the International Advisory Council of J. P. Morgan, and the San Francisco Symphony Board of Governors. She's also been awarded honorary doctorates from Morehouse College, the University of Alabama, Notre Dame, and Michigan State.

Mary Kay Ash

Through her groundbreaking company, Mary Kay Ash made it possible for millions of women to celebrate their entrepreneurial abilities while continuing to be beautiful people—inside and out. During a monthlong retirement from a direct sales career, Ash crafted the marketing plan for Mary Kay Cosmetics, then launched the company in September of 1963 with the help of her son Richard and her life savings of $5,000. A devout Christian, Ash kept family values in the forefront in business and in life along with her mission to make the world a better place for women and their families.

Ash died in late 2001, but Mary Kay Cosmetics remains one of the most familiar success stories in business, let alone women-owned business. *Fortune* magazine has routinely included the company in its list of

2003

Democrat Nancy Pelosi of California becomes the first woman to serve as House minority leader.

Sources: National Women's History Project, www.legacy98.org/timeline.html; www.gale.com

"The 100 Best Companies to Work for in America" and named it one of the ten best companies for women. The company that Ash built remains strong today, continuing its founder's legacy of providing personal and financial opportunity to women.

"Don't limit yourself," she said. "Many people limit themselves to what they think they can do. You can go as far as your mind lets you. What you believe, remember, you can achieve." Ash said she strongly identified with Martin Luther King's pointed message: "I can never be what I ought to be until you are allowed to be what you ought to be." When King spoke those words, she said, he realized that discrimination ran far deeper than skin color.

Ash spent much of her early adult life bucking female gender stereotypes and a good part of her later years helping women do the same. "So many women just don't know how great they really are. They come to us all vogue outside and vague on the inside."

Discussion Questions

1. What types of motivations are there in subjugating women and gays?

2. Who stands to benefit from marginalizing these population groups?

3. How are the two groups similar in their human rights struggles? How are they different?

Never be bullied into silence. Never allow yourself to be made a victim. Accept no one's definition of your life; define yourself.

—HARVEY FIERSTEIN

Gays, Lesbians, Bisexuals, and Transgendered People

Gay marriage continues to divide the nation in a way that few issues have. The issue became a huge political football during the 2004 presidential campaign, as eleven states passed anti–gay marriage measures and the Bush administration floated a possible constitutional amendment that would limit marriage to people of opposite sexes.

Meanwhile, polls indicate that attitudes on gay marriage are generational and that younger voters are much more comfortable with gay unions than their parents—a fact that bodes well for future social

Gay Rights Timeline

1908

The Intersexes by Xavier Mayne (Edward Stevenson) is published. It is the first American work to deal with the homosexual culture of the time. Gay resorts in New York and other cities are masked as literary or chess clubs.

1917

The U.S. Immigration Act of 1917 excludes from immigration into the United States "persons of constitutional psychopathic inferiority"—wording construed to include homosexuals.

1919

The U.S. military revises the Articles of War to make sodomy a felony.

progress for this often misunderstood, frequently maligned group.

This and other issues facing gays, lesbians, bisexuals, and trans-gendered people (GLBT) are at the heart of a debate that often boils down to "nature versus nurture"—how much of who we are is present from birth, and how much is a product of our environments. There is still a mind-set in a portion of the American population that homosex-uality can be "cured"—even as studies prove that notion a fallacy—and that heterosexuality in the context of the nuclear family is the only legitimate form of human sexual intimacy.

While mainstream culture as a whole has grown to be more toler-ant of the gay community, acceptance has been slower to come in many areas of the country—particularly in the South and parts of the Midwest. Many people in our culture unflinchingly cite Bible verses in telling gays they are "abominations," while scores of gays seek "re-verse gay counseling" and become involved in heterosexual relation-ships in an effort to suppress their sexuality.

Today many in the GLBT community must still alter their behavior

1921

The U.S. Army issues psychiatric screening regulations excluding men with feminine physical characteristics and "sexual perverts." The regulations remain in effect until just before World War II.

1924

The Society for Human Rights, the first formal U.S. gay organization, is founded in Chicago.

1927

Controversy over *The Captive*, a play with a lesbian theme, ends with the New York State Legislature's outlawing "sexual perversion" as a theme on any of the state's stages. The law remains on the books until 1967.

when in public for fear of discrimination or disapproval. Many "censor" their personal identities, introducing a companion as a "friend" instead of a partner and refraining from dancing or showing any signs of affection in public. Some even feel that they must keep silent when people in their work or social groups make homosexual jokes. From the time they start to become in touch with their sexuality, many gays are forced to feel uncomfortable in being who they really are.

When people of any group are told that their feelings aren't acceptable or natural, it's not surprising that emotional havoc ensues. The end result is often a sea of guilt, conflict, low self-esteem, and even self-hatred. Many gays link substance abuse and other self-destructive behaviors to a crushing lack of acceptance.

But the gay rights movement has made enormous progress since the American Psychiatric Association declassified homosexuality as a "mental disorder" in 1972 and the first gay civil rights legislation was introduced in Congress in 1974.

1930

A new code of standards adopted by the Motion Picture Producers and Distributors Association, spearheaded by Will Hays, states that "sex perversion or any inference of it is forbidden on the screen."

1941

The U.S. Navy issues an induction directive implicity disqualifying homosexuals. The army surgeon general issues an induction screening directive including homosexuality as a disqualifying category. The Selective Service follows suit.

1944

A military directive establishes homosexuality as a disqualification from the Women's Army Corps (WACS), clearing the way for a purge of lesbians at war's end.

Gays and the Media

While it's hard to gauge the breadth of the U.S. gay population, varying estimates have its numbers ranging anywhere from 5 percent to 10 percent of the population. Nationwide, about 600,000 same-sex partner households represented 1 percent of all coupled households in the 2000 census.

Even as this sizable community slowly assimilates into the mainstream, the portrayal of GLBTs in the media is still largely stereotypical, with a few exceptions. Gay and lesbian characters in movies and television are usually defined by their sexual orientation and generally lack any complexity.

We see the man-hating lesbians, the comically effeminate gay men, the painfully conflicted bisexuals or transsexuals. But rarely do we see healthy same-sex couples. Often, lesbian representation in movies and the media is only designed to embody heterosexual male fantasies. Transgendereds continue to be misunderstood by society

1952	1955	1958
The Mattachine Foundation, a gay rights group, mobilizes against alleged police harassment in Los Angeles.	Daughters of Bilitis, a national lesbian rights group, is founded. Its name comes from *The Songs Bilitis*, a book of love poems between women by French author Pierre Louys.	The Supreme Court rules that *ONE* magazine, the first national gay periodical, can be distributed through the mail.

and frequently appear as freakish characters who are tricking straight men into sexual activity.

Scripts frequently define gay characters by their "problems," such as sexual addiction. Although network television depictions of homosexuality are more prevalent and less judgmental than in the past, they largely remain limited to subjects such as AIDS and the characters' attempts to "come to terms" with their sexuality.

However, such cable television shows as *Queer as Folk, Six Feet Under,* and *Queer Eye for the Straight Guy* have been lauded in recent years for presenting gay people in less stereotypical contexts. But the road has been rocky. When *Queer as Folk* was in production, a half dozen major fashion houses refused to allow their brands to appear on the broadcasts. Although the plots were set in Pittsburgh, the National Football League refused to allow the use of Pittsburgh Steelers logos and merchandise for the show.

Other, edgier gay programming is cropping up. Logo, the gay cable TV channel that's an offshoot of MTV, debuted in mid 2005 with

1961	1969	1972
Illinois becomes the first state to descriminalize homosexuality.	Patrons of a gay bar in Greenwich Village in New York City fight back in a police raid, launching the Stonewall Riots.	The American Psychiatric Association declassifies homosexuality as a mental disorder.

a more mainstream emphasis than the more avant-garde subscription gay networks, Q and Here!, which have gained popularity. Retailers are also acknowledging their gay clientele. In 1994, IKEA aired a commercial that depicted two gay men shopping for a dining room set, making the store the first company to actively target gay consumers. Ten years later, Pier 1 Imports used Thom Felicia of *Queer Eye* for its TV pitchman. Other members of "the Fab Five" are seen in other marketing campaigns. The breakthrough Oscar-nominated movie *Brokeback Mountain* also went a long way in obliterating gay stereotypes.

Labels

Words used to describe offensive terminology are many: *slurs, stereotypes, pejoratives, insults, digs, slams, affronts.* But their users often have one purpose, and that is to demean others as a way of feeling superior about themselves. We see much of that dynamic at play in the way our culture references its gay members.

1974

The first gay civil rights legislation is introduced in Congress.

1977

Anita Bryant launches the antigay Save Our Children campaign. Florida becomes the first state to ban adoption by gays.

1979

Former San Francisco supervisor Dan White, invoking the "Twinkie defense," is convicted of manslaughter in the deaths of openly gay city supervisor Harvey Milk and the city's mayor, George Moscone, prompting "White Night" riots in the city.

Anybody who has spent any time around American culture knows there's no shortage of disparaging labels attached to the GLBT population. The word *queer,* once an epithet, has for the most part been reclaimed for use by the gay population and has become an acceptable term as long as it is used in a respectful manner. The terms *fag* and *faggot* are still offensive to many gays, but some gay men are reclaiming these words as well. Like *queer,* however, the words still are offensive when used as epithets.

The use of *homo, fruit, fairy, nance, pansy,* and *queen* in reference to gay males and dyke, bulldyke, carpet muncher in reference to lesbians—as well as many obscene and unprintable slurs surrounding sexual activity—are offensive across the board. Heterosexual utterances of such phrases as "That is so gay" or "You are such a fag" are pejorative. Calling someone a *DL,* or *down low,* a term for a man who has relationships with women but also has sex with men secretly, can create problems. Be careful about the joking use of the term.

1980

New York becomes the twenty-fourth state to repeal its sodomy statute.

1983

U.S. Representative Gerry Studds wins reelection as the first openly gay politician in national office.

1986

The Supreme Court refuses to extend the right of privacy to homosexual activity, ruling five to four to uphold a Georgia law that makes sodomy a crime punishable by up to twenty years.

NEVER: homo, fruit, fairy, nance, pansy, queen, poofta, fag (as an epithet) dyke, bulldyke, self-confessed gay

BE CAREFUL WITH: queer, fag, down low, drag queen

BEST: gay, lesbian, homosexual, gay men and lesbians (as a group), openly gay

Equating gays with pedophiles, or questioning their parenting abilities because of a suspicion they will try to "convert" their children to homosexuality, is not only offensive but insupportable, as both charges have both been proven false by numerous studies. (Until 1999, two prominent Web thesauruses listed the word *pederast* as a synonym for *gay* before removing it in the face of multiple complaints.)

When there is a legitimate need to define a person's sexuality, the

1987	1989	1993
Two thousand gay and lesbian couples are "married" in a mass mock wedding outside the Internal Revenue Service building in Washington.	Denmark allows same-sex couples to register their relationships.	President Clinton seeks to lift the ban on gay military service. As a compromise, the "Don't ask, don't tell" policy is adopted.

acceptable term for a male homosexual is *gay*. For females, *lesbian* is preferred although *gay* is acceptable. In referring to both, use the term *gay men and lesbians*. Most transvestites prefer *cross dresser* to *drag queen*, when publicly referenced, although the latter is not offensive to many. The term *openly gay* is much preferred over such guilt-implying descriptions such as *self-avowed, self-admitted,* or *self-confessed.* "

Leaders

Barney Frank

Until the 1980s, gay politicians and other public figures remained closeted for the most part. However, Representative Barney Frank, the most prominent openly gay politician in the United States, disclosed his sexuality seven years after his election to Congress in 1981. A Harvard Law School grad, he has represented the Fourth District of Massachusetts ever since. The Democrat has been a gay rights activist most

1994

The American Medical Association opposes medical treatment to "cure" homosexuals.

1996

A Hawaii court overrules the state gay marriage ban, prompting national concern that leads Congress to overwhelmingly pass the Defense of Marriage Act, which is signed by President Clinton. The act denies recognition of and benefits to partners in same-sex marriages. The Supreme Court strikes down a Colorado amendment that had prohibited statutes or policies barring discrimination against homosexuals. A U.S. appeals court upholds the military's "Don't ask, don't tell" policy.

1997

Speaking to the Human Rights Campaign, a leading gay rights group, Clinton becomes the first U.S. president to address a gay and lesbian organization. Hawaii extends many marital benefits to gay couples.

of his adult life and has been outspoken on other human rights issues.

In 1995, Dick Armey, then House majority leader, referred to Frank in an interview as "Barney Fag." He apologized and claimed the slur was just a slip of the tongue. Accused of pushing a gay agenda, Frank, the ranking Democrat on the Financial Services Committee and a member of the Select Committee on Homeland Security, said his only "agenda" is a set of long-term goals to "make people free to pursue their own nature without suffering the legal discriminations."

Capitol Hill staffers routinely give the energetic Frank, who serves on the Subcommittee on Infrastructure and Border Security and the Subcommittee on Intelligence and Counterterrorism, the title of the "most intelligent" Democratic member of the House of Representatives, as well as its funniest member (Washingtonian.com, 2004).

Frank sees a trend of tolerance emerging in the United States: "I think what happened is that Americans discovered that they weren't antigay, they just thought that they were supposed to be," he said in a lecture at Georgetown University.

1998

The Georgia Supreme Court strikes down the state sodomy law, saying it violates privacy rights guaranteed by the state constitution. Two men are charged in the beating death of openly gay University of Wyoming student Matthew Shepard, renewing debate nationally on hate-crime laws. Voters in Hawaii and Alaska approve initiatives defining marriage as a heterosexual union, thereby banning same-sex marriages.

1999

The Vermont Supreme Court orders the state government to offer homosexual couples the same benefits and legal rights afforded to heterosexual married couples. Clinton uses a recess appointment to name openly gay James Hormel as ambassador to Luxembourg after his confirmation is blocked by Republican senators.

Frank has helped give gay politicians across the country the courage to disclose their sexuality. In 1991, there were only 49 openly gay politicians in the United States. By 2002, there were 223 openly gay politicians, according to the Gay & Lesbian Victory Fund.

Ellen DeGeneres

Comedian Ellen DeGeneres had already built up a cult following when she rose to national attention in April 1997, coming out of the closet on both her sitcom, *Ellen,* and in real life. As one of the first openly gay performers playing an openly gay role, she suddenly found herself cast in the role of activist and role model.

DeGeneres appeared on the cover of *Time* with the headline, "Yep, I'm Gay," and was quoted as saying that she "never wanted to be the lesbian actress. I never wanted to be the spokesperson for the gay community. . . . I did it for my own truth." Following her very public "outing," DeGeneres won civil rights awards for her efforts from the Human Rights Campaign and the American Civil Liberties Union of Southern California.

2000

The Vatican's Pontifical Council decries efforts to give unmarried partners the same legal rights as married people. General Motors, Ford, and DaimlerChrysler offer full health-care benefits to the same-sex partners of their full-time salaried employees, the largest such program offered by major U.S. corporations.

2000

The Supreme Court rules five to four that the First Amendment allows the Boy Scouts of America to oust a homosexual scout leader in New Jersey. Vermont gives same-sex couples the same legal rights as heterosexual married couples.
A Defense Department survey finds harassment of gay soldiers commonplace and tolerated in the military.

Since that time, she played a lesbian in the short-lived *The Ellen Show*, before launching the popular daytime talk show *The Ellen De-Generes Show*, which won four Daytime Emmy Awards in its freshman season, including Best Talk Show.

George Takei

Japanese American actor George Takei, known best for his role of helmsman Hikaru Sulu on the USS *Enterprise* in the classic TV series *Star Trek*, revealed in late 2005 that he was gay and had an eighteen-year committed relationship with his partner, Brad Altman. He said the disclosure (in *Frontiers* magazine, October 2005) was "not really coming out, which suggests opening a door and stepping through. It's more like a long, long walk through what began as a narrow corridor that starts to widen."

After the original *Star Trek* ended its TV tenure, Takei ran for mayor of Los Angeles in 1973, finishing second to then City Council-man Tom Bradley in a field of seventeen. He later served on the board of directors of the Southern California Rapid Transit District to help

2001

A federal judge upholds the Florida law banning homosexuals from adopting children, in the first federal court decision on the issue.

2002

New York becomes the thirteenth state to add gays and lesbians to its antidiscrimination law.

2003

The Supreme Court, acting on a Texas case, overturns sodomy laws still on the books in thirteen states, calling them an invasion of privacy. Canada and Belgium follow the Netherlands in officially recognizing gay marriages. U.S. gay couples flock to Canada to wed.

plan the Los Angeles subway system, performed in *Star Trek* movies, cowrote a science-fiction novel, guest-starred on several TV shows, published his autobiography, *To the Stars,* and spent eight months playing psychiatrist Martin Dysart in Peter Shaffer's theater classic *Equus.* In 2006, he became the official announcer for Howard Stern's Sirius Radio show.

On his blog, Takei says he and partner Altman "will continue to speak out for gay and lesbian equality in 2006 and beyond."

Issues

There is still a lot of work to be done on the legislative front for America's gay population. Although more companies are offering health benefits for same-sex companions, they are often not the equivalent of the benefits extended to legally married employees, because access to such benefits is contingent on civil marriage or union. That is a right that's still denied to gay and lesbian couples in many states, regardless of the longevity of their relationship.

2004

Gay marriage becomes an election issue. Massachusetts legalizes same-sex marriage in May, while eleven other U.S. states ban the practice through public referenda in the November elections; domestic partnerships in New Jersey are legalized in July. In Canada, 85 percent of the population now lives in a province or territory with same-sex marriage. Texas becomes the thirty-seventh state to adopt a defense of marriage act, denying recognition of same-sex unions formed in other states.

2005

California extends some marriage rights to same-sex couples.

Even when companies offer domestic partner benefits to same-sex partners of gay men, lesbians, and bisexuals, they are often taxed as income by the federal government, while spousal benefits are not—an inequity that causes economic hardship to many lesbian- and gay-headed families.

Gay marriage is now legal in America's neighbor to the north, Canada, and in Spain, the Netherlands, and Belgium. Other countries are considering it. Many feel this trend can only lead to the eventual liberalization of laws in the United States.

When Illinois acted to ban antigay discrimination in 2005, it was estimated that 47 percent of the U.S. population, or 138 million people, lived in a jurisdiction that banned discrimination on the basis of sexual orientation, according to the National Gay and Lesbian Task Force Policy Institute. Ten years prior, that figure was 34 percent.

But that still means that 156 million Americans, or 53 percent of the population, live in a jurisdiction or state where because of their real or perceived sexual orientation, people can be fired, refused ser-

2005

On June 29, the Canadian parliament passes a bill legalizing gay marriage throughout the country. On June 30, Connecticut becomes the second state to offer civil unions to same-sex couples, granting them many of the rights and privileges of married couples. It's the first state to do so without being forced by the courts. The law includes an amendment that defines marriage as being between a man and a woman.

Source: Len Evans, The Gay Chronicles, www.geocities.com/gueroperro/GayChronicles.

vice in a restaurant, denied housing, or turned down for a loan, simply because they are gay.

Gays have faced decades of discrimination. In 2002, one official for a group called Concerned Women for America criticized the homosexual lobby for "co-opting the black civil rights struggle," adding that the National Gay and Lesbian Task Force's agenda of "promoting perversion—including public homosexual sex, sadomasochism and bisexuality—that would offend the vast majority of African-Americans who understand the difference between God-designed racial distinctions and changeable, immoral behavior."

But in a speech to a national gay rights organization, Coretta Scott King, the wife of the late Dr. Martin Luther King Jr., said that homophobia "is like racism and anti-Semitism and other forms of bigotry in that it seeks to dehumanize a large group of people, to deny their humanity, their dignity and personhood." She said homophobic attitudes and policies were "unjust and unworthy of a free society and must be opposed by all Americans who believe in democracy."

Whites Are Not Immune to Labels

Prejudice is a two-way street. You don't have to be a person of color to be labeled. White members of the gay, bisexual, and transgendered communities and the disabled community can attest to that, as can white citizens who have faced age discrimination in employment.

The truth is, no group is exempt from labeling. It's still common for whites without a bigoted bone in their bodies to be stigmatized as "racists" or "entitled" based on old assumptions. Though the days when the controlling white class systematically denied privileges to nonwhites have faded, many of the labels associated with that era remain active, particularly among those who refuse to advance their thought processes with the changing times.

During this country's dark era of discrimination, many whites were often treated as second-class citizens by other whites, particularly Irish Catholic laborers who fled famine and hardship in their home country only to be marginalized and mistreated when they arrived on American shores.

In recent decades, affirmative action programs have promoted charges of so-called "reverse racism" and perpetuated hostile labels among both whites and people of color in the process.

Although the word *honky* has largely disappeared from the American vernacular, it has been replaced by more common use of the word *cracker* or *cracka*. Various historians speculate the slur originated from a Scotch-Irish term that meant "boastful person," or a "corn cracker" making moonshine, or worse, a "whip cracker." In some minority communities, *cracker* is sometimes used as a pejorative term synonymous with *white trash*. Though often used in self-jest, the word is generally a slur. It and terms such as *Casper, whitey,* and *poor white* can be offensive.

(cont.)

The term *redneck* can be a pejorative to some and a matter of regional pride to others. But it is often used to imply that a person is a "hick" or "hillbilly" or a racist and should be used with caution. Many newspapers that refuse to print other slurs still use *redneck*. The word *WASP,* an acronym for "White Anglo-Saxon Protestant," plus the Jewish term *goy,* meaning "non-Jew," are considered slurs to many whites.

Yes, whites are targets of labels too. Bias crosses all demographic boundaries and is kept alive by living deeply in the past. (Sometimes we just need to stop and realize that we are much more like our most recent ancestors than our more distant ones.) Racism can only die when we stop stereotyping individuals based on their physical traits and the tired old labels of the past.

TEN

People with Disabilities

I've learned that it's not the disability that defines you, it's how
you deal with the challenges the disability presents you with.
And I've learned that we have an obligation to the abilities we
do have, not the disability.

—JIM ABBOTT, RETIRED
ONE-HANDED PROFESSIONAL BASEBALL PLAYER

Unlike other minorities, the disabled are not united by class or ethnic distinction and are often left out of discussions on diversity. But disability is an equal opportunity condition, encompassing a diversity of mobility impairments, visual and hearing impediments, mental illnesses, learning disabilities, autism, and long-term or chronic illnesses such as cancer, diabetes, epilepsy, and AIDS.

Unlike any of the other groups we have studied, accidents, sudden sickness, or aging can land any of us in the disabled category at any time. Depending on what's considered a disability, the number of disabled Americans ranges from 35 million to more than 45 million at any time. Some are born with conditions that we label disabilities; others may acquire one or more through accident or illness. In fact, many of us, if not most, will develop some form of a disability in our elderly years. The baby boomer generation, of which I am a member, will soon be the senior set.

Like other population groups outside the mainstream, there is little question that the disabled have suffered discrimination. In a shameful period of our nation, the "eugenics" movement of the late 1800s led to passage in the United States of laws that not only prevented people with disabilities from moving to this country, marrying, or having children, but also led to the institutionalization and forced sterilization of many of our citizens. However, disability itself doesn't discriminate. It encompasses all ages, races, sexual orientations, and both genders.

Since the start of recorded history, we know that people with physical and mental challenges abounded in the world. An ancient sacred poem of India, the *Rig Veda,* is the first record of prosthesis use. Written in Sanskrit between 3500 and 1800 BC, the poem recounts the tale of a warrior, Queen Vishpla, who was fitted with an iron prosthesis after losing a leg in battle. The fitting enabled her to return to combat.

Through much of our history, stereotypical attitudes have portrayed individuals with disabilities not only as different but as deficient or even aberrant, giving rise to the now archaic word *invalid,* meaning "not valid." One of the earliest identifiable organizational responses to a disability was the creation of asylums or "special schools" to contain people with various afflictions.

In some respects, that attitude is still pervasive. In scenarios not unlike what befell many minorities in our country, particularly Native Americans and African Americans, children with disabilities are often labeled at a young age and shunted into special classes until they are deemed "normal" enough to join the mainstream. Meanwhile, their friendships and social lives are limited, as they have been conditioned to think that they don't belong and cannot lead fulfilling lives.

When the authors of the Declaration of Independence wrote that "all men are created equal, that they are endowed by their creator with certain unalienable rights, that among these are life, liberty and the pursuit of happiness," were they excluding people with disabilities?

The author of the essay "People First Language," Kathie Snow, has said that all groups are represented among people with disabilities, actually making it the largest minority group. And the one thing this group has in common with the others is dealing with societal prejudices, discrimination, and misunderstanding.

In truth, disability, like ethnicity and gender, is just one more aspect of the human condition. When we ask ourselves how we would like to be treated or defined if we were to develop a disability, our answers probably indicate how those with disabilities currently would want to be treated. That is, as a person—not as a statistic or an object of pity, or as someone who is merely defined by his or her lack of mobility or other impairment.

LABELS

By focusing on the person and not the disability in our speaking and writing, we foster a more respectful and inclusive attitude toward persons with disabilities and help remove those many labels and stereotypes that are built on fear and ignorance.

Many words that were once acceptable in describing the disabled are now considered insensitive and hurtful. Among them are *cripple* or *crippled, lame,* and the above-mentioned *invalid.* The words *handicap* and *handicapped* should no longer be used to describe a person or disability, although they can be used freely when citing laws.

Words like *crip* or *gimp* or *palsied* and *bent* are insensitive and usually intended to demean. Instead of *deaf and dumb* or *deaf mute,* use *deaf person* or *hearing impaired.* Words for the mentally ill such as *crazy, mental patient, insane, mad,* and *deranged* are inappropriate. Casually saying "That is so retarded" to a friend can be hurtful to mentally retarded persons or their guardians and relatives.

Feel free to use *persons with disabilities* or *people with disabilities, disabled persons* or *disabled people* when it is necessary to identify a group.

Above all, don't make people feel as if they belong to a disabled community. It is very isolating. Referring to groups of the disabled as "the retarded" or "the blind" has that impact. Instead of *wheelchair bound,* use *wheelchair user.* Instead of calling a person a "paralytic" or "arthritic," simply say "person who is paralyzed" or "person with arthritis."

Be careful with the terminology *afflicted with, stricken with, suffers from,* or *victim,* because they reinforce a victim complex and are isolating. For example, an "AIDS victim" should just be a "person with AIDS." The phrases *differently abled* and *physically challenged* aren't offensive but are a little condescending.

> NEVER: *cripple, lame, invalid, gimp, palsied, deaf and dumb, crazy, insane, the retarded, the blind, afflicted with, wheelchair-bound, victim of, AIDS victim, freak, midget*

> BE CAREFUL WITH: *handicapped, differently abled, physically challenged*

> BEST: *persons with disabilities, people with disabilities, disabled persons, disabled people, person who is paralyzed, wheelchair user, person with AIDS*

People with Disabilities

1809	1817	1832	1841
Louis Braille is born near Paris. Blinded at three years of age in an accident, Braille is sent in 1819 to the Paris Blind School, an institution founded by Valentin Hauy.	Considered the first school for disabled children in the Western Hemisphere, the American School for the Deaf is founded in Hartford, Connecticut.	The first two students, sisters Abbey and Sophia Carter, are admitted to Boston's Perkins School for the Blind.	A new publication, *The American Annals of the Deaf,* is issued in Hartford, Connecticut.

And quit staring! While disabled people—particularly those using assistive devices—are accustomed to curious people, you can probably sense where to draw the line. Acknowledge a disabled person as you would any other person. On the other hand, don't snap your head away and pretend you don't see. You can't imagine how hurtful this is unless you have been there.

Avoid the "tragic but brave" stereotype when you are writing about the disabled. Many of the disabled don't feel as if the simple act of dealing with a barrier or a condition is heroic. They do not want pity.

LEADERS

Famous people with disabilities include several leaders you have already read about in these pages, including Harriet Tubman, who as a slave was struck in the head by a white overseer for refusing to help tie up another slave who had attempted escape. As a result, Tubman lived with narcolepsy the rest of her life, although she still managed to help three hundred slaves to freedom in the North through the network known as the Underground Railroad.

1848	1854	1864
Over the next century, hundreds of thousands of developmentally disabled adults and children will be institutionalized, many for life. The first residential institution for people with mental disabilities, the Perkins Institution, is founded by Samuel Gridley Howe in Boston.	Montpelier, Vermont, sees the founding of the trailblazing New England Gallaudet Association of the Deaf.	President Abraham Lincoln signs the Enabling Act, which gives the Columbia Institution for the Deaf and Dumb and Blind authority to award college degrees, making it the first such educational institution in the world established exclusively for people with disabilities.

Native American leader Wilma Mankiller became principal chief of the Cherokee Nation in 1985, six years after being diagnosed with a rare form of muscular dystrophy. She was the first woman to hold such a high-ranking position in a major tribal government. World War II hero Daniel Inouye, whose right arm was amputated after it was shattered by a grenade in combat, has served seven terms as a U.S. senator from Hawaii.

Stephen Hawking

Few people have been known to accomplish more in the face of physical adversity than Stephen Hawking, who was diagnosed with amyotrophic lateral sclerosis (ALS), a motor neuron disease, as a graduate student at Cambridge. He has become one of the world's leading theoretical physicists and is considered by many to be the most brilliant person since Albert Einstein. Since 1979, he has held the esteemed position of Lucasian professor of mathematics at Cambridge University—a post once held by Isaac Newton.

Hawking refuses to be trapped by fate. After completely losing the use of his vocal chords in a 1985 tracheotomy procedure performed to assist his breathing, he has communicated through a computer and speech synthesizer, enabling him to lecture around the world and author several

1869	1878	1880
The first U.S. patent for a wheelchair is registered with the U.S. Patent Office.	Joel W. Smith presents his Modified Braille to the American Association of Instructors of the Blind. The association rejects his system, continuing to endorse instead New York Point, which blind readers complain is more difficult to read and write.	"Oralism" advocates at the International Congress of Educators of the Deaf in Milan call for the suppression of sign languages and the firing of deaf teachers at all schools for the deaf. The move is seen by advocates for the deaf as a cultural attack on the deaf community.

books. His best seller *A Brief History of Time*, has been translated into thirty-three languages and has sold close to 10 million copies.

Once asked how he felt about being called the world's smartest person, the self-effacing Hawking said, "They just want a hero, and I fill the role model of a disabled genius. At least I am disabled, but I am no genius." On his Web site, Hawking said he tries to lead as normal a life as possible, "and not think about my condition, or regret the things it prevents me from doing, which are not that many."

Two of the world's other great minds also had disabilities. Thomas Edison was challenged by a hearing impairment, and Einstein had dyslexia.

Lance Armstrong

Legendary American bicycle racer Lance Armstrong could have been counted among the disabled during his bout with testicular cancer, which eventually spread to his brain, lungs, and abdomen. In 2005, he cycled his way to an unprecedented, and perhaps never-to-be-equaled, seventh straight Tour de France victory before "retiring" from road racing.

Armstrong has become a symbol of strength and hope for cancer survivors worldwide as well as a highly visible spokesman for the cause. As of

1883

The term *eugenics* is coined by Sir Francis Galton in England to describe his theory about improving "the stock" of humanity. A eugenics movement becomes the catalyst for laws preventing disabled people from moving to the United States, marrying, or having children, and it also leads to the forced sterilizing and institutionalizing of many disabled adults and children. Eugenics campaigns against immigrants and people of color also lead to passage of "Jim Crow" laws in the South and additional immigration restrictions.

1887

Anne Sullivan meets Helen Keller for the first time in Tuscumbia, Alabama. Sullivan immediately begins training Keller to "finger spell."

2006, the sale of his Livestrong wristbands have helped the Lance Armstrong Foundation raise more than $50 million for cancer survivorship programs.

Christopher Reeve

Christopher Reeve, best known for his starring roles in four *Superman* movies, worked tirelessly on behalf of the disabled after suffering an injury in 1995 that left him a quadriplegic. Both a stage and screen star, Reeve found his life changed in seconds when he was thrown headfirst from his horse during an equestrian competition in Virginia. The impact broke two upper vertebrae in his spine, leaving him paralyzed from the neck down and able to breathe only with ventilator assistance.

After a six-month recovery period, Reeve resolved that his condition would not define him. He quickly mastered the art of talking between breaths of his ventilator and soon became proficient at using a specialized wheelchair operated by blowing puffs of air into a strawlike control device.

He set about fulfilling a new set of objectives, one of which was to increase funding for spinal cord research with the ultimate goal of finding a

1890s–1920	1901	1902	1908
Activists push for the creation of state worker's compensation programs. By 1913, twenty-one states have established some form of worker's comp. The figure rises to forty-three by 1919.	The National Fraternal Society of the Deaf is founded in Flint at the Michigan School for the Deaf. For a half century, the society fights for the rights of deaf people.	The first deaf and blind person to enroll in college, Helen Keller, publishes her acclaimed autobiography, *The Story of My Life*.	An exposé on deplorable conditions found inside state and private mental institutions, *A Mind That Found Itself* written by Clifford Beers, is published.

cure for paralysis. He also made numerous public appearances on behalf of the disabled, serving as master of ceremonies at the Paralympic Games and delivering an emotional opening-night speech to the Democratic National Cenvention in 1996.

Late that year, Reeve went back to work, serving as the voice of King Arthur in the animated feature *The Quest for Camelot* and later making his directorial debut in the HBO movie *In the Gloaming*, which was about a family struggling to cope with the impending loss of a son to AIDS.

Reeve was shrewd enough to parlay his celebrity status into millions of dollars of financial support for spinal cord injury research. He also intensified the lobby for insurance reform, helping increase the lifetime benefits cap for catastrophic injuries and illness from $1 million to $10 million in many plans. He founded the Christopher Reeve Foundation, which raises funds for biomedical research, and served as chairman of the American Paralysis Association.

Reeve, determined to walk again, made amazing progress that allowed him to move his head, shrug his shoulders, and spend hours at a time off the respirator. But he never quite realized his dream, dying of

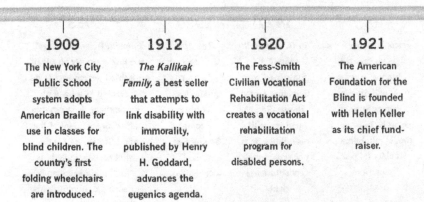

1909

The New York City Public School system adopts American Braille for use in classes for blind children. The country's first folding wheelchairs are introduced.

1912

The Kallikak Family, a best seller that attempts to link disability with immorality, published by Henry H. Goddard, advances the eugenics agenda.

1920

The Fess-Smith Civilian Vocational Rehabilitation Act creates a vocational rehabilitation program for disabled persons.

1921

The American Foundation for the Blind is founded with Helen Keller as its chief fund-raiser.

heart failure at age fifty-two in late 2004 while directing *Yankee Irving*, an animated feature film. However, he gave hope to others in his situation; many benefit from his efforts. "So many of our dreams at first seem impossible," he said. "Then they seem improbable, and then when we summon the will, they soon become inevitable."

Michael J. Fox

Actor Michael J. Fox, known for his *Back to the Future* movies and starring roles in the *Family Ties* and *Spin City* TV comedy series, was diagnosed with early-onset Parkinson's disease in 1991. He would not share the news with the public until 1998. But it didn't take him long to progress from hiding his disease to becoming an eloquent spokesperson about it.

Since leaving *Spin City* in 2000, Fox has helped raise or fund more than $52 million through his Michael J. Fox Foundation for Parkinson's research. "Nobody would choose to have a disease visited upon them," he has said. "Still, Parkinson's forced me to make a fundamental life decision: adopt a siege mentality—or embark upon a life journey." Now Fox

1927	1927	1929	1933
Franklin Roosevelt's newly created Warms Springs Foundation in Warms Springs, Georgia, becomes a model rehabilitation facility for polio survivors.	In *Buck v. Bell*, the U.S. Supreme Court finds that forced sterilization of persons with disabilities does not violate their constitutional rights.	The first U.S. school to train guide dogs for blind people, Seeing Eye, is established.	Franklin Delano Roosevelt, the first seriously physically disabled person ever to be elected as a head of government, is sworn into office as president of the United States. He continues what he later called his "splendid deception," choosing to minimize his disability so as to appear "able" in the eyes of the American people.

talks about the disease without a hint of self-pity and even demonstrates a gratefulness for life he says he had never experienced before.

Fox and other high-profile people with disabilities, including the late Christopher Reeve, have vigorously pushed to relax restrictions imposed by President George W. Bush in 2001 on embryonic stem-cell research on human embryos, which holds promise in the search for cures for Alzheimer's, Parkinson's, diabetes, certain types of cancer, and other diseases.

Even as his illness continues to progress, Fox remains active with his foundation and continues to guest-star on TV series and lend his voice to animated movies. He seemed to speak for all persons with disabilities when he recently said publicly, "One's dignity may be assaulted, vandalized, and cruelly mocked but cannot be taken away unless it is surrendered."

Like other good leaders, Fox has helped transform people's understanding.

There are literally hundreds of other famous people who have lived, or are living, with disabilities. Here are just a few:

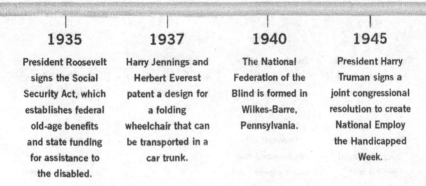

1935	1937	1940	1945
President Roosevelt signs the Social Security Act, which establishes federal old-age benefits and state funding for assistance to the disabled.	Harry Jennings and Herbert Everest patent a design for a folding wheelchair that can be transported in a car trunk.	The National Federation of the Blind is formed in Wilkes-Barre, Pennsylvania.	President Harry Truman signs a joint congressional resolution to create National Employ the Handicapped Week.

Ludwig von Beethoven, deafness

Stevie Wonder, blindness

Ray Charles, blindness

"Magic" Johnson, AIDS

Greg Louganis, learning disability/AIDS

Danny Glover, epilepsy

Marlee Matlin, deafness

Mary Tyler Moore, diabetes

Julius Caesar, epilepsy

Winston Churchill, learning disability

Franklin D. Roosevelt, polio

Richard Pryor, multiple sclerosis

1946	1946	1948	1949
Congress authorizes federal grants for the construction of hospital and other public health facilities for the rehabilitation of people with disabilities.	The Cerebral Palsy Society is established in New York. The National Mental Health Foundation is established and helps expose poor and abusive conditions at mental-health facilities.	The Paralyzed Veterans of America founds the National Paraplegia Foundation.	The National Foundation for Cerebral Palsy is established. The first annual Wheelchair Basketball Tournament is held in Galesburg, Illinois.

Itzhak Perlman, paraplegia

John Milton, blindness

Ronald Reagan, hearing impairment/Alzheimer's disease

Wilma Rudolph, post-polio syndrome

Lou Gehrig, ALS

ISSUES

Despite progress spurred by the Americans with Disabilities Act (ADA), our country still denies some of the most basic rights to the disabled—albeit not intentionally in most cases.

In the 2004 election, thousands—perhaps tens of thousands—of Americans may have been unable to vote because hundreds of polling places were not accessible to people using wheelchairs or walkers. In Missouri, for example, nearly a quarter of polling places were inaccessible to disabled voters, a survey conducted for the secretary of state's office

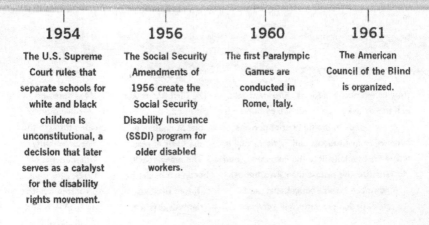

1954	1956	1960	1961
The U.S. Supreme Court rules that separate schools for white and black children is unconstitutional, a decision that later serves as a catalyst for the disability rights movement.	The Social Security Amendments of 1956 create the Social Security Disability Insurance (SSDI) program for older disabled workers.	The first Paralympic Games are conducted in Rome, Italy.	The American Council of the Blind is organized.

showed. Of those that were accessible, nearly half had at least one significant barrier to voting for the disabled. Other states reported similar problems. In fact, the Federal Election Commission estimates that as many as twenty thousand polling places across the nation are still inaccessible, in violation of federal and state laws. Polling booths are often in church basements or in upstairs meeting halls with no ramp or elevator access. Some have too-narrow doorways or no disabled parking spaces.

And many states still don't offer Braille ballots, so people with severe vision problems have to bring someone along with them and trust that they will vote as instructed. In other words, a person requires sight to have the right to a secret ballot.

Because of the difficulties, many disabled persons just stay home on Election Day rather than face potentially embarrassing situations. They are in effect deprived of their most basic right to influence policy that will affect them.

There has been much progress, however, in incorporating the disabled into the mainstream. Depictions of disabilities in the media and movies are growing more progressive as such industry watchdog groups as the Media Access Office, which promotes employment of the disabled in

1963	1964	1965
In a congressional address, President John F. Kennedy asks for a reduction by hundreds of thousands in the number of persons confined to institutions, calling for means to return the mentally ill to the community and to revitalize and restore their lives through advanced health, educational, and rehabilitation programs and services.	The Civil Rights Act outlaws discrimination on the basis of race. The measure will become a model for future disability rights legislation.	Medicare and Medicaid are created through the Social Security Amendments of 1965, providing subsidized health care to elderly and disabled Americans.

TV and film, assert themselves. Also, there are now more disabled performers in general.

Much of today's awareness of the disabled population grew out of the independent-living movement and the refusal of many of our disabled Vietnam veterans to be shut away in institutions. They asserted their right to live independently and to be treated with respect, and many advocacy services grew from this model.

While we still see some stereotypical or overly sentimental characterizations in the media, the recent films *I Am Sam,* about a mentally retarded single father trying to gain custody of his young daughter, and *A Beautiful Mind,* based on the true story of Nobel Laureate John Forbes Nash Jr., a math genius with schizophrenia, have both been lauded for their sensitive portrayals of the disabled.

It's a long education process. Positive attitudes can be shaped through more discussions and presentations in schools and corporations about people with disabilities.

Remember that people with disabilities are not broken. They are complete human beings who simply happen to have specific physical or mental challenges that most others do not. People with disabilities just want us to see the ability, not the disability. When you address the disabled and all people of dif-

1966	1968	1973
The President's Committee on Mental Retardation is established by President Lyndon Johnson.	The Architectural Barriers Act mandates that federally constructed facilities be accessible to the disabled. The Urban Mass Transportation Assistance Act states that elderly and handicapped persons have rights to mass transportation and should be physically accommodated to board.	Disabled activists protest the veto of the Rehabilitation Act of 1973 by President Richard Nixon.

ference with dignity, you become not only an example setter, but a facilitator of change and a true leader.

Discussion Questions

1. Where do persons with disabilities fit in during discussions on diversity?

2. How does modern society's response to disability differ from earlier models?

3. How do you think persons with disabilities feel about their role in mainstream society?

1973	1981	1981–83
Handicap parking stickers are introduced in Washington, D.C.	An "International Year of Disabled Persons" is declared.	The Reagan administration threatens to amend or revoke regulations implementing the Rehabilitation Act of 1973 and Education for All Handicapped Children Act of 1975. Intense lobbying efforts and grassroots campaigns generate thousands of cards and letters of protest; the administration abandons its efforts.

1981–84

The Reagan administration terminates Social Security benefits for hundreds of thousands of disabled people to reduce the federal budget. Telecommunications for the Disabled Act mandates telephone access for hard-of-hearing people at public places.

1985

The Supreme Court rules that localities can't use zoning laws to prohibit group homes for the developmentally disabled from opening in residential areas.

1987

Deaf actress Marlee Matlin wins an Oscar for her performance in *Children of a Lesser God.*

1987

The U.S. Supreme Court outlines the rights of people with contagious diseases under the Rehabilitation Act of 1973, establishing that people with infectious diseases can't be fired because of "prejudiced attitude or ignorance of others." The landmark ruling establishes protections for people with HIV/AIDS and other infectious or noninfectious diseases or disabilities who are discriminated against out of fear.

1990

The Wheels of Justice campaign brings hundreds to the nation's capital in support of the Americans with Disabilities Act (ADA). Activists are arrested when they refuse to leave the Capitol rotunda. The Americans with Disabilities Act brings full legal citizenship to Americans with disabilities for the first time, mandating the accessibility of local, state, and federal facilities. Businesses with more than fifteen employees are required to make reasonable accommodations for the disabled.

1991

The Ryan White Comprehensive AIDS Resource Emergency Act is passed.

1995

The American Association of People with Disabilities is founded in Washington, D.C.

1996

Congress eliminates more than 150,000 disabled children and substance-dependent people from the Social Security rolls.

1996

Bob Dole becomes the first presidential candidate with a visible disability since Franklin Roosevelt.

1998

A Supreme Court ruling expands the Americans with Disabilities Act to include persons with asymptomatic HIV and disabled people incarcerated in state prisons.

1999

The Supreme Court rules that people whose conditions do not substantially limit their life activity and are easy to correct are not to be considered disabled under the ADA.

2001

The Commonwealth of Virginia House of Delegates apologizes for its eugenics practices from 1924 to 1979.

2005

The feeding tube of Terri Schiavo, who suffers from
irreversible brain damage, is removed. She dies at
a hospice where she lay for years while her
husband and parents fought one another in the
nation's most heavily litigated right-to-die dispute.
The U.S. Supreme Court refuses to intervene.

Sources: Fred Pelka, The ABC-CLIO Companion to the Disability Rights Movement, Santa Barbara, CA:
ABC-CLIO, 1997; Disability Social History Project, Disability History Timeline,
www.disabilityhistory.org/timeline_new.html.

SECTION 3

Transformation

ELEVEN

Leaders Not Labels

Leadership can be thought of as a capacity to define oneself to
others in a way that clarifies and expands a vision of the future.

—EDWIN H. FRIEDMAN

You move from a label to a leader by freeing yourself from limitations, by
busting out of your box.

When you've reached that point, labels cease being a consideration.
Every time you hear one, you ignore it or sidestep it. It doesn't resonate
with you. When you take that tack every day, you are authentically transforming into a leader.

*We've found that if you don't engage the world from your strengths—your
talent and skills—you engage it from your weaknesses.*

As human beings, the strongest thing we have is our spirit. If you're
living a life based on weakness, you become vulnerable and very susceptible to having your spirit broken. And when your spirit is in distress, a
negative spirit prevails and keeps you from having a spirit of cooperation.
When that happens, you can't lead yourself and you can't lead others.

In Orange County for the launch of the new Tiger Woods Learning
Center, I stood alongside my lifelong friend Carl Rustin, who came from

the same background as I did. During the technology tour of this amazing facility, we were marveling at a toy, suspended on a string in front of us, that was made up of little plastic components. It was traveling back and forth like a trolley car on its own momentum. I said, "Carl, if we saw that when we were growing up, what would we have done?" He didn't hesitate. "We'd grab that thing and throw it against the wall and break it into pieces," he said. I quickly agreed. That thinking came from a time before we each had developed a spirit of cooperation—before we had turned destructive thoughts into constructive ones.

Later, as I was driving around the area on a beautiful day, I was struck by how attractive, cohesive, and progressive the area was. There were blocks and blocks of neatly constructed buildings and beautiful landscapes. Businesses were inviting. Commerce was brisk. Tasteful new development was springing up everywhere. The hotels and homes and parks were quaint and thoughtfully designed. People were walking and bicycling around their community, gathering in cafés and shops and obviously enjoying themselves.

Negativity wasn't the least bit apparent, as it is in so many other cities and counties I visit. It was obvious that if outsiders came into town and caused a problem or disruption, the city would try to push them out as soon as possible. The residents would do this based on their vision, their desire to go in one direction—a positive one.

Then it struck me: the reason they can do this is that there is a spirit of cooperation here. Money alone can't make that happen. These folks are all heading in the same direction because they share a vision.

When you don't have that vision and that spirit of cooperation, you can't build anything of substance. You can't make your own vision happen. That spirit of cooperation is the opposite of negativity and cynicism, the opposite of not loving yourself and the others who try to share your space. Without it, you can't create a beautiful, cohesive place. You can't build an Orange County of the mind.

When you're negative, your space is so small that precious few people can occupy it with you. But when you're positive, and when you have a smile on your face and you are open and able to deal with all kinds of people and situations, you're really focusing on love. You are looking for the love and the goodness in people of all races and persuasions. You are leading.

When you reach that point, you find yourself able to excel and create opportunities and to focus on what you can do, as opposed to what you can't do. You create more opportunities and build momentum for constructive growth, just as in a model city.

When everyone is going in the same direction, whether in a city, a company, a school, or a family, it's usually because a leader has created a spirit of cooperation. In a classroom, if you have one or two disruptive students, they can take the whole classroom in a different direction. You don't have that spirit of cooperation you'll need in the long run. Leadership is subverted.

If you don't like yourself, if you only focus on your weaknesses, then you won't harbor that spirit of cooperation. You can't be open to other people and opportunities because you still haven't developed your own internal spirit of cooperation.

Under those circumstances, it's hard to realize how important it is to try your best and build as much value into your life as possible—in other words, to love yourself as much as you can. The educational system doesn't teach you that. It teaches you how to memorize and take tests and regurgitate information. A few days later, it'll label you with a grade. A few weeks after that, you may not remember a thing you "learned" for the test.

We live in a world where most people do the same thing over and over every day. They get into a routine and a rut. So many of them, after about thirty years of doing the same thing, look back and say, "I have no more as my life winds down than I had in the beginning." So if you do today the same thing that you did yesterday, that you did last year and years before that, what have you done? Nothing.

So what is the missing equation? It boils down to five letters: *T-H-I-N-K*. Sometimes we forget to turn on our brains. Sometimes we keep them in the off position so long, we become complacent. We get so busy tending to our daily rituals that we do nothing new. Soon, we stop growing. And if you don't grow, then your goals stay the same.

You can be fifty or sixty or seventy-five years of age and still have never grown. You're still talking about the same things, still doing the same things, using the same mind-set. You end up limiting yourself, and the only way you hope to stay afloat is to tread water in that one area where you do have influence. And that may be a *very small* area because you lacked growth. For example, you can't leave that job because that's the only job you've ever known; you can't leave town because that's the only town you've ever known. And if you do somehow manage to escape your surroundings, you'll soon realize how much things are changing in the world, and you may not be able to adjust.

DIVERSITY AND GROWTH

So the question becomes, How do you build that much-needed foundation for growth?

You start by taking more control of your life and becoming more accountable to yourself.

You begin to understand how much better it is to be able to take all the information available to us and make it relevant to your own personal and professional development. You incorporate it into your own world and add your own twist. You take ownership of it. This frees you to come up with your own ideas and integrate them. When you do this, you are able to reinvent yourself every day and organize your life around the world, instead of just allowing the world to organize itself around you. You are leading instead of being led. You are willingly expanding your horizons and becoming flexible enough to continue to grow.

In a nutshell, that's what diversity is all about: broadening your outlook and being inclusive. That's why I wrote this book—to illustrate how to transform your true value and authenticity as a person into an asset and connect with the rest of the world.

When you choose this path, you automatically become more flexible; you learn more; you do more and you *are* more—based on your potential. There are other side benefits. You become less jealous of others, less concerned about what they're doing, and you break the habit of judging and prejudging people. In fact, you become more accepting of them because you've decided to become more accepting of yourself.

When we don't know who we are, then the world defines us by our exterior things, by our house, our car, our appearance—and our race. Millions of people of color around the country and world believe that they can't make it because of their skin color. They're programmed to believe that they're second-class citizens. And how are second-class citizens expected to act? That's easy: they act out the role of second-class citizen.

Essentially, they're giving their power over to somebody else to define them as human beings. This can happen to people in every walk of society, regardless of their status, color, or orientation.

Many of us continue to be defined by our parents and the messages we got growing up. A lot of these messages were negative. The real challenge is to break away from that negativity and the preconceived notion of who you've been told you are, based on a label that they or someone else close to you has given you.

The educational system is not set up to teach this kind of emotional and social transformation. It does, in theory, teach you math and science and other technical information. But if you don't get that, you end up without a degree. And if you don't get your degree, then society says you're not worth that much.

Sometimes you buy into that degree label and fail to seek out a pursuit that is your true calling. Of course, degrees are essential in practically all walks of life today. But you change; your degree doesn't. A degree doesn't always tell others—or even you—who you are as a person.

More than ever, we are so confused by the complexity of our world that it's almost impossible to keep up with the many micro details and issues that bombard us daily as we try to determine what is substantive and credible and what isn't. The world is evolving at the same time that it's being broken into a billion tiny pieces. We have a great many niche and segmented markets in our professional lives, and very many distractions in our personal ones. It is getting progressively harder to get a handle on all this information and all the obligations, issues, and challenges that are being hurled at us by the world. They too can be a box if we let them and can't prioritize.

But the truth is, you can go as far as you want, if you piece together all those things—your education, your true passion, and the wealth of information available on the Web and in the world—then apply that to your own life based on how you see yourself. To use a boxing analogy, a fight is often won before it starts. The real battle is the rigorous training and discipline the fighter exercised before jumping in the ring. Training and preparation always set the stage for success.

THE LEADERSHIP EDGE

There's a verse in Proverbs: "Where there is no vision, the people perish."

How important is leadership? It is absolutely essential—in every sense. A lack of leadership can make the difference between the life and death of an idea, an organization, a person, a family, or even a population. Every day, we see the results of poor leadership at home and abroad. In business, we continue to see the demise of many organizations that have fallen into leadership famines.

Often, cultures create leaders by turning over power wholesale to them to determine that culture's identity and its destiny. It doesn't matter that these marginally qualified leaders may have no long-term vision for the future or not be worthy of the leadership role they hold. Those who put them there will still feel compelled to follow, as will others who are taken in by the impulse to join the rest of the crowd. But they are not necessarily following a true leader. They are following a title. Too often in the business world, these leaders' cultures are about immediate gratification and how much money can be made *right now.* It's tempting for these leaders to think in the short term because they want to wring out a quick profit and run. Sometimes that path leads directly to jail.

Leaders with a big-picture view know that to keep their edge in the global marketplace, they will need an adjustable long-range plan. They know their plan will always include a diverse workforce offering a wide range of backgrounds and perspectives and worldviews to reflect the cultures and communities where they do business, whether that's in Anytown, USA, or in multiple locations around the globe.

It's no coincidence that business leaders who are the most active in diversity tend to be constantly engaged in self-examination, looking deeply inside their company as well as outside for fresh answers and new talent. They are not satisfied where they are. For them the name of the game is to stay in the game.

This is a time in our world when innovative and effective leaders are desperately needed to cope with all the input. Good leadership is about being able to execute when it's critical to execute; it's about making your programs happen, about galvanizing people and pulling them in. Unfortunately, not everybody had the right role models around to start the leadership process and build their foundations when they were growing up. I was lucky to have parents who challenged me to transcend my circumstances.

But they couldn't think for me. It took me a long time to own my own life instead of having someone else define me. When you don't own yourself, you are allowing others to categorize and label you, and you always end up coming away with much less than those who did the defining. If you give away that personal control, you are just acquiescing to a set of policies you're expected to live under.

Labels have their own rules, support systems, outlines, and expectations.

Government policies are created on them, platforms are built on them, and wars are waged on them. These labels have their own physical and psychological barriers that you only cross at your own peril.

As we've illustrated in our historic examination of people of color, with gender diversity, and with disabilities, some labels have been around for hundreds of years, sometimes thousands, and are often embedded deeply in the national psyche.

As the world changes, a new breed of diverse leadership is asserting itself in corporate America. And it asserts itself more in attitude than in process. "Leadership is not a formula or a program, it is a human activity that comes from the heart and considers the hearts of others," says Lance Secretan, a fellow organizational motivator.

Leadership and achievement, it seems, all come back to change. The best leaders are also the best at change. It used to be that leadership meant telling people what to do, and then putting fear in their hearts if they didn't perform. Today leadership is more about being nimble, reacting quickly to the market and motivating and inspiring people to sustain a progressive and fluid organization.

Leadership is about motivating people to take action to get the job done. People are willing to respond to the right call: they long to be challenged. The most cutting-edge leaders are capable of seeing past their current circumstances to create positive changes to evolve with the times. As Jesse Jackson, one of America's best-known facilitators of change, puts it, "Time is neutral and does not change things. With courage and initiative, leaders change things."

Most leaders have followers because they were first able to lead themselves. They built their own foundation for leadership by thinking independently: they've engineered their own life brand. Like our great leaders, they are carried to the top by others who see their potential. They, in turn, lift as they rise.

EXPANDING YOUR FIELD OF VISION

When you have attained your personal vision, you too will develop a clearer vision for your community or your civic organization or your company. More important, you will be self-owned, and that's an achievement you can always savor because you earned it through your hard work and unique talents, not from a figurehead or a faceless organization that doesn't know you—yet is all too willing to slap a label on you.

Consider the Hindu proverb: *"There is nothing noble about being superior to some other man. The true nobility is in being superior to your previous self."*

As you can see, asking you to become a leader, not a label, is more than a call for political correctness. It is a wake-up call for you to look more deeply into yourself, so you can in turn look more deeply into others. When you see yourself for what you are, it's easier to see others for what they are—not for what you want them to be. It's also a call for the retirement of the old prescribed view of "normalcy." It's a plea to destroy that old label you've been serving under and abandoning those labels you put on others.

Personal leadership, in the end, is about finding out who you are based on your talents. It is about working as hard as you can to find out your uniqueness as a person and what you bring to the table. It is about growth and transforming into a better person. It is this process that has freed me and given me a sense of self-transformation. I don't have to focus on all the little, petty negative things, as I did in my high school days back in New Jersey—on all those things that kept me from transforming until later in life.

What's most important is to break through those labels and get to the spirit of the human being—elevating yourself based on who you are, and who others are, as unique people. When you accomplish that, you become a true leader to yourself, to others, to the marketplace, and to the world.

TWELVE

The Nine Steps:
Transform and Thrive

Let us all hope that the dark clouds of racial prejudice will
soon pass away, and that in some not too distant tomorrow the
radiant stars of love and brotherhood will shine over our great
nation with all their scintillating beauty.

—MARTIN LUTHER KING JR.

I've dedicated my life to teaching a nine-step process for personal and
professional transformation because I think it's a great way for individuals
to grow from who they are to who they can be. That foundation is very important because it can motivate continuous improvement for those willing to focus on their core bases.

There are two distinctly different blueprints for your core base: internal and external. Unfortunately, many of us never get to examine the internal one—the real core of who we are—because we are too busy
focusing on the external.

Sure, you may spend ten minutes every so often thinking about what
you're doing with your day and your life while you're driving to and from

work, but that's not much reflection. If I were to ask several people, "How much time do you spend with yourself every day?" the answer would most often be "A few minutes—maybe." And that's a shame, because it's important to find that time to think about who you are and how you should plan your life around your core foundation. The less you do this, the less control you have over your life. Meditation, prayer, exercise, and quiet reflection all help you nurture the core. But there's a specific set of building blocks for this transformation—the nine steps—that can help walk you through this process of introspection and core building every day.

That's important, because without that introspection and self-direction, the world will tell you, "If you're not going to control yourself, I'm going to control you; I'll be the master and *you* be the slave." That's how you get into a pattern of doing things everybody else wants you to do and virtually nothing that truly nourishes you.

Often people feel as if they're doing what they want to do when they're actually doing something the external world has programmed them to do, and that is to be a consumer. For example, when people treat themselves to a new dress or new suit or an expensive electronic gadget or a car, they feel as if they're nurturing their inner beings. What's really happening is that they have been persuaded to buy all these external things that make it look as if they're really doing something with their lives. They are buying into somebody else's vision. We waste an astounding amount of time buying into things that aren't relevant to who we are.

Truth is, about 1 percent of the population leads the world and everybody else just follows. The reason we have so many followers is that they don't know how to build their foundations from the core out; they don't know how to direct themselves based on their points of strength.

The nine-step building process is designed to help you sustain that leadership-building process daily in this fast-moving world and free you from your old constraints so that you can also become a leader in society—not someone's label.

THE NINE STEPS

Step 1: Check your ID

I do seminars with young people, and I often call four or five of them up to the front early on and say, "OK, you've got thirty seconds to name everything that you love." Most of them can list several things and people pretty quickly. Some come up with as many as twenty-five to thirty-five in that half-minute window.

That's because everybody knows what they love. When you focus on what you love and what you do well and what you respond to, then you've started the process of building who you are. You are checking your own ID.

There's a saying: "Don't let your pain be the design for your life." That's a pretty profound perspective on self-definition. I have my own saying: "You aren't your circumstances, you are your possibilities." That means that you can create a life based on your possibilities, on being positive, enjoying what you do and having the energy and motivation to address it every day. The beautiful thing is that it doesn't make a difference what your background is, or how bad your personal and professional histories were, or how bad your circumstances were; you can overshadow those with all the positive things in you that are based on your passions— your love. It doesn't mean you'll forget the negatives in your life. It just makes them less significant than the positives.

Motivation is critical to the success of this process, because without motivation you can't get up in the morning and stay on the job all day. Without motivation, you can't be excited about what you're doing or go about overcoming obstacles when you're tired. For those exercisers who feel too washed out to work out on a given day but do anyway, you know what I mean. You realize the value exercise brings to your life and know you'll get into it once you start. You're advancing a positive process even when the tough times come. That resolve applies to any worthwhile pursuit.

Looking at our school systems, many of our students aren't motivated because their attentions lie elsewhere in so many outside distractions. The classroom and teachers and course become passé to students, and it gets harder and harder for them to become excited about arts and language and science because they're too stimulated by outside things. The external world has them in its grip. They grow accustomed to all the temptations and tastes and toys within their reach, and they just want more and more and more of them.

But when you don't have the self-discipline and awareness about where you're going or who you're going to become, you are really going to end up with less and less. You can't focus on your passions and core base, and you become more susceptible to doing things that make you feel good but have no genuine relationship to who you are and who you need to be.

This check-your-ID step is so critical because if you don't take it, if you don't focus your life on building your passion. Then you end up being average and doing average things with average people, with average results. You go through the motions because you have to, not because you're meant to.

If you look at all the people who are really successful and happy, they're doing exactly what they want and love to do; they are self-actualized.

Though some of us start out with more opportunities than others, what really makes us all equal in the pursuit of self-identification is one thing: we all have twenty-four hours. What makes us unequal is that some people use their twenty-four hours for productive growth, while other people don't—in effect giving away their twenty-four hours. The question comes back to this: What do I do with my own twenty-four hours? It doesn't make any difference if I'm a teen or if I'm seventy-five years of age or disabled. There is still time for me to do what I love.

Something a friend of mine said to me in recent years really stuck. "We're starting to get up there!" he said, as we talked about aging. I agreed. Then he added, "I guess you just do the best you can every day." That summarizes it, I thought: Do the best you can every day.

But how do you go about doing the best you can every single day? You have to ask yourself, how do I just divide up those twenty-four hours so I can get the best possible results out of my day?

Well, if you can align that step with who you are—your ID—and know exactly where you're going, then you're well on your path.

Step 2: Create Your Vision

Having a vision moves you out of your current circumstances. If you stay in the same place in your life, then it stands to reason that you're not going very far. In fact, you may already be at your final destination, performing the same routine for the same people. There's nothing wrong with a routine: a routine gets results. But it usually gets the same results. To grow, you want different results.

The way to get those different results is to develop a different perspective, a new vision of your possibilities. Vision is a road map. Vision is a guiding light. Vision is your ability to see beyond your current circumstances. Vision puts you in the future. When things get tough and you're caught up in the moment, dealing with all the everyday "stuff," your vision can carry you beyond that moment. It says, "Yes, I'm going to have to suffer through this because, based on my vision, I know that things are going to get better."

Creating your own vision gives you a tremendous advantage. It's analogous to climbing a mountain. You know that you're not going to be able to ascend the mountain in a straight line. There'll be trails—probably several. There will be rocks and other obstacles and seemingly impassable areas that you will have to go around or over. The process requires one sure step at a time. As you progress, the mountain will get steeper and steeper and steeper, and you'll leave a lot of people behind. You have a vision of the top of that mountain, and you know where you want to go. When you get there, you'll look back down at everyone else below you. Some will have quit the climb and others will have been content to make it only halfway up.

A vision helps you get to the top. It helps you see the whole picture and not just a small piece of it. Vision allows you to innovate, create, develop, to see the possibilities and dream the dream. But to implement that dream, to climb that mountain, you've got to be organized and be prepared. That's where the third step comes in handy . . .

Step 3: Develop Your Travel Plan

Now you must develop a plan to actualize your vision—to make it a reality in your life. How can you accomplish this?

You'll need significant exposure to your passion, of course. Good old-fashioned fact-finding and dedication about this area of interest will give you an edge in developing your personal travel plan. It would be advantageous to find a mentor or someone else who can help you see the evolution of the things in your professional world far beyond where they currently stand—someone to help you expand your mind and think big, a colleague or friend; someone who is living his or her passion. Absent that, you can still execute your plan using the incredible wealth of resources available to you. There's no shortage of information, especially with the millions of Web sites and blogs and the plethora of specialty publications created for every industry. Your research is only limited by your imagination.

The next step in developing your travel plan is to tailor your goals and routine to those day-to-day functions that you'll need to achieve—the goals that will help you achieve your vision. The size of your vision, of course, will determine how big your plan is. If you have a large vision, then your plan will have to be as large as that vision. Take on something manageable to start, but with a bigger picture always in mind.

After that, you'll have to prepare to execute your vision. It's one thing to create a vision; it's another thing to implement it. If I truly desire to make it to the NBA, then I have to execute my program every single day with that goal in mind. I have to ask myself, "How will I use those twenty-four hours to work toward that vision?" I've got to fine-tune my jump shot, I have to practice on all phases of my game, I have to lift weights, I have to work on my vertical jump and my speed. I need to be superior, because I am talking about being among the best in the world. That goes for every profession or objective for which you strive. Every day you must ask yourself, "Where do I want to go with it? Do I want to be the supervisor in my division? Do I want to be a manager, based on what I'm doing? Do I want to be an officer of this company someday? A CEO?" Your long-term plan needn't have limitations.

It's how you break that process down into pieces that will dictate your success. We live in a world where we're dealing with all kinds of new segmentation and niches and an influx of people from the farthest reaches of the country and the earth. There's a lot to sort out.

Segmentation is a powerful part of your travel plan. It is about pulling together all kinds of diverse components. It's about being able to organize everything you do into small pieces—and figuring out how you're going to manage those small pieces to get the most value out of each, while constructively changing the whole. If you put all those pieces together, then that vision allows you to build your own culture. And the beautiful thing about organizing a culture is that when you do, you have the best information and resources and experts for that culture at your fingertips to help you build value in each of those areas. This added value helps you take your travel plan on the road as you create your unique "brand."

Your brand is how you stand out, how you convey your uniqueness and position yourself in the marketplace so that you'll have more added value than competitors. It's a crucial element of your plan. In a previous book, *Build Your Own Life Brand*, we talked about investing in yourself and how your internal and external elements combine to equal your maximum potential.

Branding is not to be confused with advertising. Advertising is merely communicating to the public who you are after you become what you are. Branding gets you where you're going. Your brand needs depth and substance—and a distinct vision. It's what you'll be known for. It's a consistent effort based on who you are and what you're doing every single day.

Vision allows you to be a mile long and a mile deep. It lifts you above the expectations of others, beyond the labels you're given. It puts you on the highway.

Step 4: Master the Rules of the Road

These rules are your guiding principles on that road, that value system you've created that's based on your personal vision of who you want to become. Your personal rules of the road need to include guiding principles such as commitment, honesty, and hard work to go with your vision and travel plan.

Under these rules, hard work and commitment won't seem nearly as daunting if you're focused on your passion and heading in a direction that's tied to your purpose and your values. You will be propelled by your own force.

You'll discover that "hard work" is really a numbers game. It's about repetition and doing more than the next person. I liken it to doing sit-ups or push-ups. You decide how strong you can be and how far you can take this. This is about your will and execution and overcoming barriers of physical and mental fatigue, and the work you're willing to put in. It's about doing more than the competition. What's your threshold?

The intensity of your vision often determines your work ethic and spells out the rules of the road. Vision sets the tone for how much time and effort you're going to put into something to make your unique talents blossom.

Tiger Woods says he's not good just because he was born Tiger Woods; he's good because he practices twice as hard at his passion than everyone else. So when you think about executing your travel plan, know that success is about going that extra mile. If you want to be great at something, you have to work twice as hard as the competition.

It also comes back to sustainability. You can't sustain yourself over a long period of time in something you don't feel passion for. You simply burn out. That's why some people with an intense passion can work up to sixteen hours a day if need be: they love what they do. It's that energy that is driving them and making them stand out. They may not be the most talented at their craft, but they are getting the most results out of what talents they do have to offer. And when you do that, the world responds. People are looking for leaders, not followers.

When we talk about becoming a leader, not a label, it sometimes boils down to one question you have to ask yourself: "Am I going to be a leader, or am I going to be a follower?"

Determination and perseverance are a couple of hard-and-fast rules of the road. You may not be the strongest, the smartest, or the sleekest, but if you hang in there long enough, the scenery will change and the road will become less crowded. Are you still going to be in the race five years from now? Ten years from now? It all depends on your level of determination. If you can align your determination and perseverance and priorities with your passion, you'll have staying power in what you do. You'll be a natural.

Of course, it's not always apparent what your passion is. Often, through a process of elimination, you can figure out early on what it is you *don't* want to do. You may have to experience a variety of options as you search for answers and possibilities. But you can't let yourself fall into a comfort zone or a rut of someone else's making.

Staying positive through the race is another hard-and-fast rule of the road. A study conducted by Dr. Masaru Emoto and reported in his book *The Hidden Messages in Water* showed that water crystals are transformed according to the positive and negative thoughts to which they were exposed. Negative emotions, he found, kept water from crystallizing, while positive emotions allowed it to develop into exquisite shapes. The same holds true in humans. Negativity keeps us from crystallizing.

As an athlete in basketball, my goal was to break the spirit of the team we played. When I and my teammates saw the fear in our opposition's eyes, we knew we had them. The world can do that to you as well; it's constantly trying to take you out of the picture. There'll be people who try to categorize you. They'll try to limit you and label you and diminish you—in order to break your spirit and control you.

But you have to stand fast and not let the world define you. You have to build strength every single day based on having a positive life. How do you develop such strength? And how can you eliminate the negative in your life to build that vision and achieve your purpose? By following two other rules of the road: stay focused and stay positive.

When you focus on your purpose and your passion, you'll lose interest in the things that can drag you down, sap your energy, and steer you from your objectives. People in a work environment respond favorably to positive people. They may convey some negativity and have other bad habits, but in the end, they will respond to people who are moving in the right direction. Attitude is altitude, as they say. Those allegiances will allow you to build value and create opportunity based on their skill sets as well as your own.

When you hear yourself saying, "I worked fourteen hours today, but I'm pumped," you're there. You never want to lose that. You've come to realize that your life and your work truly matter and that you've found a place where you're consistently happy. You can face all the obstacles because you know they're not going to take you out of the race—or off the road.

Step 5: Step into the Outer Limits

That's a big step, but you can only take it if there's not a big emotional force holding you back.

When you break it down, there are two basic emotions: fear and love. How big is fear in our lives? In too many of us, it's bigger than our own life. As we look back to examine where that fear came from, we learn a lot about ourselves. To some degree, we were all taught fear—at least enough to protect us. Many of our fears are, or were, tied to our belief systems, which largely stemmed from our parents as well.

You might look back at your upbringing and think, "Which parent did I learn that habit from?" Certainly, many of our moms and dads parented negatively. That's just one perspective you may gain as you revisit your history—in order to move into your future. But it should not be a blame-laying visit. Most of our parents did the best job they could with the information they had. If they'd known better, they'd have done better. I found a lot of good but also some bad in my own upbringing, and I've consciously strived to separate myself from the bad while retaining all the good. I came to realize that I had to if I wanted to move my life away from my youth and into the realities of the twenty-first century. And doing this was a technique that allowed me to stay in the now and create a life based on my possibilities, not on how I was programmed by my parents. Our parents, after all, were programmed by their parents too.

This work enabled me to create what I wanted in life based on who I am and my own vision, not who I was when I was growing up. That's a very powerful thing. We can't allow ourselves to stay permanently locked in our old fear-based vision. We can create a new vision of our own, then another and another. There is no limit.

That's what we mean when we say we are stepping into the outer limits. It's a process that demands that we step away from our old inner limits and re-create the world based on our possibilities and resources.

When you change your thinking, you change your possibilities. It doesn't happen overnight. It's a process that involves taking small steps, and it's a lifelong journey. You've heard of fear of success, which at face value seems a bizarre notion. But we are programmed, by ourselves and others, to believe that we're not supposed to be successful. We draw close to success and then sabotage ourselves, putting up our own roadblocks—before shrinking into the role of "victim." It is the personification of fear-based thinking. "I can't go in to work this morning. I can't do this. I'm a fake. What if I fail?" That's fear. It's a conscious or subconscious effort to stay in your old comfort zone and retreat from the world.

There's another major fear at play here: fear of the unknown. As long as you stay in the same space—that box—you'll never have to face it. But you won't grow either. Maya Angelou has said, "Courage is the most important of all the virtues because without courage you can't practice any other virtue consistently. You can practice any virtue erratically, but nothing consistently without courage."

Stepping into the outer limits is being able to say, "Hey, you know what? I'm just going to keep going, even though I'm afraid I'm just going to take that risk. I'm going to take this promotion. I'm going to move out of my hometown and take that challenging job across the country."

These steps not only have encouraged me to overcome my own programmed fears, they have taken the color and race elements out of the equation as well. For me to be able to expunge these fear-based and race-based thoughts from my day-to-day decision making was a gigantic step in my evolution as both a businessman and a person.

Now when I ask myself questions such as "What's the process for building a business?" "What's the process for writing a book?" or "What's the process for accomplishing my goals?" I do so without all the tired old labels and biases clouding my judgment. I simply bypass the places where people who try to put me in a box tell me, "You can't do that." I step out and away from that box, into my own outer limits.

Before I could take that step, I examined how I was programmed and what belief systems I bought into. The process showed me how to get from where I was to where my possibilities were. It disproves the notions that you can't make it because of the color of your skin, or because you're a woman living in a man's world, or because your family doesn't have enough money, or because you came from the wrong side of the tracks.

That is why moving out of your history and into your own imagination is so important; that's why literature is so important, why reading and research are so important. They expose your possibilities and take you further than where you are—toward your outer limits.

Ninety percent of winning is simply believing that you're supposed to win because you're doing the best job you can every single day. "If you don't believe it, you can't achieve it," the saying goes. Sure, you may not have all the resources or support you'd like right now. But your belief system is what will keep you in the game or in the race. It says, "I'm going to hang in there regardless of my circumstances." Soon you'll bypass the naysayers and followers and all the others who accept programming that tells them they are not good enough and move into a leadership position because that's where you wholeheartedly believe you're supposed to be.

I think everybody in the world is supposed to be a king or queen. I think that's what we should all aspire to, based on our purposes and passions. But if you don't start that process of building a foundation, the game won't stop and wait for you. Maybe you have been on this journey for forty-five years and still haven't started the process of building anything. You're just existing and struggling to survive every day, and the external world owns your mind and your soul—because you let it.

But it is never too late to start to seize back that power that will finally allow you to venture into your outer limits.

Step 6: Pilot the Seasons of Change

We're going through countless changes today in technology, with the advent of the global economy and the assimilation of so many different populations into our society. Increasingly, we're becoming one people. We've been in a war where most of us have learned more about the cultural nuances of the Middle East and Muslims than we ever thought possible. There are always threats of new war, riots in France, world summits, cultural changes in Africa and South Africa, shake-ups in the United Nations, a "New World Order," and hundreds of thousands of people taking to the streets of America to make their voices heard.

As conditions change rapidly, people are changing mind-sets. They're becoming more and more knowledgeable about their possibilities to survive in the new economy. Students are expressing their dissatisfaction with how countries are governed and with the status quo. They're challenging those systems and trying to take more control of their own lives and future. Our leadership today promotes an ownership society while the president and other politicians ponder the fate of the Social Security system. Companies are cutting pensions, and today's younger generation is facing the prospect of having less to rely upon for retirement. Those under fifty are being told that they will have to invest in their futures: the government won't be capable of it. This change comes at a time when people are living longer. They're not focusing on retiring at sixty-five anymore—or even retiring at all. They're looking at ways to reinvent themselves based on new career ideas, new technologies, new opportunities, and their own longer life spans. We continue to see a growing gap between the haves and the have-nots. Those who know how to access the system are able to use it for their own benefit. Those who don't are left on the sidelines.

As we talk about focus and passion and ownership and freedom, there's never been a better time to free your thinking and reorganize your focus. But what is that focus?

I teach seminars and workshops to corporate clients. As I gazed across the room at the one hundred or so people present at one session, I noticed that they came from a wide range of backgrounds: Asian, Hispanic, African American, Middle Eastern, mixed ancestry, a balance of men and women. You couldn't possibly categorize them all, I thought. And why would you want to?

Clearly, the workforce doesn't have time to build barriers anymore or proffer special treatment based on race. You'd go broke trying to "save" all these cultures from the rest of the world. People everywhere have to transform; they have to pilot the seasons of change themselves. They have to rise above. They have to be able to focus not on their races but on what they do well and what they bring to the table.

We're moving into such a talent-driven ownership society that businesspeople don't have the time or desire to care about color. The business world can't afford to care about your background or where you came from. *You* have to care about that.

You will come to see your own culture as a celebration of your life, to focus on what in it is relevant to you, opposed to giving someone else the responsibility to preserve your cultural integrity. People are looking for value and talent, and that search is becoming color-blind.

These steps can allow you to build from your strengths and passions, to help you focus on what your mission is and what you should be doing with your life. They can also help you shed your thin skin. Adapt and be open enough to say, "I'm going to hang in there and not change my core every time change happens. I will organize what's relevant to my own purpose and my own development. I will be steadfast yet receptive. I will pilot those seasons of change."

Step 7: Build Your Dream Team

There's a saying that no one makes it alone, that people are not islands unto themselves. We all need some kind of team. Why not build your own dream team?

You can't make it by yourself, but many of us try. Why? Often it's because we've spent years mired in a survival mode, just doing things that the world wanted us to do. Hence, nobody really wanted to join us; we were out there by ourselves—renegades—pursuing activities that had no connection to growth or building.

But when you take some chances and develop your plan based on your passion, when you take that big step out, you'll be looking for a like culture and like people to join you—people who are going in the same direction based on the second step: vision.

To build your team, you need to utilize existing channels and networks to advance your agenda in the marketplace. That network—your "team"—will be critical. Some team members will be people who work with you. Others will be family members, organization members, association members, or community members. Whoever they are, the team members will relate to what you do and to your core base and vision.

Can you build your team based on your purpose? How do you get into some of those good ol' boy and good ol' girl clubs? How do you open other doors to find people who will help you drive that mission and purpose? How do you get people to respect you and admire what you do because you do it so well? How do you create that magical spirit of cooperation among your peers? How do you get promoted to a position where you can better build your dream team?

It all starts with liking yourself first and being able to get along with people and treating them the way they want to be treated, not the way you want to treat them. Find out what they do best and make them feel good about who they are. Then you'll attract teammates, and those questions will slowly be answered as you move forward.

How do you make people feel good about themselves? That's all part of leadership. Leadership used to be about putting fear in people's hearts: "If you don't do this, you're going to get fired." But because we're moving into a talent-driven society, leadership is more about motivating people than about striking fear into them. It's making people feel good about themselves, not yelling at them. It's also about creating freethinkers and self-starters who are willing to learn and get to the next level, not about looming over people and micromanaging them to death.

In this sense, leadership is also about getting people engaged, getting them to learn about your organization, your company, your business, so that they are able to suggest new ideas and new ways of doing things to contribute to the growth of the company. I often say in lectures, "If you're a weak person, you'll have a weak team. If you're a strong person, you'll have a strong team."

Funny thing: you don't pick your team members; they pick you. That's why vision is so important. People are not going to seek you out if you don't have strong vision and a strong core base, or if you don't know where you're going and can't separate yourself from the rest of the crowd.

If you can't build a team, then you're not going to be considered a leader. If you can't lead yourself first, you can't build that leadership foundation. If you can build a foundation, you can grow and attract quality teammates who will help you fulfill your vision.

Step 8: Win by a Decision

Life is about the choices we make. We've all made good and bad choices. Many times, we just weren't armed with the information and perspective to make the good ones.

It could be that your parents were poorly educated or abused as children, or your siblings may have gone astray. That background makes it harder to make the decisions to build a firm foundation.

Our choices are based on how we see ourselves in the world, whether we believe in ourselves and what kind of examples we've had. I see a lot of young people today who simply aren't equipped with the information they'll need to thrive in this world. They don't get it on the front end, so they suffer on the back end. A lot of them don't finish school. And they realize as they grow into adults that maybe they should have stuck around.

Our decisions determine our fate. If you hadn't called someone a name, you wouldn't be in a lawsuit. If you hadn't told that supervisor what you think of him, perhaps you'd still have your job—a job that might have led to greater things in a profession for which you seemed a natural. If you had waited until you found another job before you quit your current one, maybe you could be paying the rent.

Winning by a decision in your life goes back to clarity—clarity on who you are, where you're going, and how you're going to get there. Many times we miss out on a great opportunity because we weren't clear on those things and the opportunity just passed us by.

Winning by a decision is making the choice to be successful. I used to be the class cutup throughout grade and middle school, high school, and even college. One day I looked at myself and my funnyman role and decided it wasn't getting me anywhere. I decided I needed to change the way I dealt with folks. Then they would change the way they dealt with me.

That choice was a defining moment in my life. It eliminated a lot of the negative, distracting things in my life and allowed me to get more serious about developing my talents and building my future. I began the process of reestablishing myself based on who I wanted to become. Those were choices. So is success.

Step 9: Commit to Your Vision

Commitment is not just doing something; it is a lifestyle. You have chosen something that is near and dear to your heart to commit to—something you're very passionate about that will sustain your interest for a long time.

Commitment asks the question, "Can you hang in there, and if so, how long?" It's a pledge to something you believe, something that you want to keep as an important part of your life and an important part of who you are. It's a piece of your program, your essence. And you need to work on fulfilling that commitment every single day.

But that's not an easy thing to do. You've got to stay with it and demonstrate the perseverance to sustain it. It is your vision and you must nurture it.

I spend a lot of time in planning and preparation to fulfill my vision and create the life I enjoy. I do a lot of soul-searching and ask myself the right questions: "How do I contribute to my industry? How do I maintain consistency over a long period of time? How do I provide as much support as I can to those people who are in my life? How do I eliminate things that are not relevant to my decision making? How do I take care of myself and eat the right foods and find the energy to exercise when I feel tired? How do I balance my travel and work schedule with my personal life?"

In this changing, global society, you will have to be more introspective, more focused, more streamlined; you'll have to be able to move on a dime. You can't get pulled into every little external conversation or petty problem. You have to ignore all the time wasters, who may be trying to pull you in the wrong direction. You've got to remain focused and clear on where you're going and how you're going to get there.

Commitment to your vision is a full-time job, and you have to constantly seek out ways to achieve your goals and your vision based on what you want to do and need to do.

I hope you have enjoyed reading this book, and that it has inspired you to realize that we are all unique, yet the same. Our successes and failures are based on a clear understanding of our potential and how we develop the uniqueness that determines who we are. As the saying goes, "This is a journey, not a destination." We must keep trying to grow and be open enough to learn. Moving from labels to leaders is no easy task, but finding the freedom to reach your potential makes it worth it. This is going to be the requirement of the twenty-first century.

Index

About the Author

Stedman Graham is chairman and CEO of S. Graham and Associates (SGA), a management and marketing consulting firm based in Chicago. He is the author of ten books, including two *New York Times* bestsellers, *You Can Make It Happen: A Nine-Step Plan for Success* and *Teens Can Make It Happen: 9 Steps to Success*. He lectures and conducts seminars for businesses and organizations around the country, and clients have included Merrill Lynch, Wells Fargo, Hyatt Hotels Corporation, Manpower, and CVS Pharmacy.

Graham is a former adjunct professor at the University of Illinois in Chicago. At the Kellogg Graduate School of Management at Northwestern University, he taught a management strategy course entitled "The Dynamics of Leadership." In 1985, he founded AAD Education, Health and Sports, a nonprofit organization of 500 athletes and other civic leaders committed to developing leadership in underserved youths. AAD has served over 15,000 students and has awarded $1.5 million in scholarships.

Graham serves on several boards, including the national board of Junior Achievement (JA) and the 7-Eleven Education Is Freedom Foundation. He is also a member of the Economic Club of Chicago. Graham holds a bachelor's degree in social work from Hardin-Simmons University, a master's degree in education from Ball State University, and an honorary doctorate in humanities from Coker College, where he is also a distinguished visiting professor.